D0638369

Date Due

ROMAN CATHOLICISM

HUTCHINSON'S UNIVERSITY LIBRARY

CHRISTIAN RELIGION

EDITOR:

REV. PROFESSOR E. O. JAMES,

M.A., D.LITT., PH.D., D.D., F.S.A.
*Professor of the History and Philosophy of Religion
in the University of London*

ROMAN CATHOLICISM

by

THOMAS CORBISHLEY,
S.J., M.A.
MASTER OF CAMPION HALL, OXFORD

1950
HUTCHINSON'S UNIVERSITY LIBRARY
Hutchinson House, London, W.1.

New York   *Melbourne*   *Sydney*   *Cape Town*

THIS VOLUME IS NUMBER 51 IN

HUTCHINSON'S UNIVERSITY LIBRARY

Printed in Great Britain by
William Brendon and Son, Ltd.
The Mayflower Press (late of Plymouth),
at Bushey Mill Lane
Watford, Herts.

IMPRIMI POTEST: M. C. D'Arcy, S.J.,
Praep. Prov. Angl.

NIHIL OBSTAT: H. Franciscus Davis, S.T.D.,
Censor Deputatus

IMPRIMATUR: ✠ Joseph,
Archiepiscopus Birmingamiensis
Birmingamiae, die 23a Aprilis, 1949

CONTENTS

INTRODUCTORY

THIS book is an attempt, on the part of a Roman Catholic, to state what he conceives to be the nature and function of the Church to which he belongs. As far as possible it avoids controversy, though when we are dealing with an institution which has been and is the object of continual criticism and even misrepresentation (however unconscious), it will be necessary, for the sake of clarity, to touch on controverted points. The Roman Catholic believes that his creed is capable of reasoned statement and defence; he is not less aware that other factors besides rational analysis must come in to produce conviction. Those who read the book are asked to believe that what it contains is set down in all sincerity and honesty. It is difficult to write with entire detachment about fundamental truths, involving the most precious values; nor can an institution which is primarily religious be analysed with the scientific rigour applicable to some purely social or political organisation. It is true that Roman Catholicism is often regarded as a purely temporal phenomenon. Any attempt so to regard it is doomed to failure. It can only be appreciated by those who are prepared to make the effort to judge it from the standpoint of its adherents.

May I, at this point, say a word about the book's title? I have agreed to write about 'Roman' Catholicism not because I regard the qualifying adjective as free from objection, but because it is in possession. To object to it at this stage must savour of discourtesy or pedantry. At the same time I should like to ask my Anglo-Catholic friends to extend the same tolerance to me when I seem to use the term 'Catholic' in a sense which they might not altogether approve.

The reason, of course, why the prefix 'Roman' finds no favour with those to whom it is applied is precisely because it is liable to misinterpretation. The 'Roman' Catholic holds that his Church is alone truly Catholic in the sense of being truly universal—universal not in any mere geographical sense, not alone in the sense that she claims to direct her appeal to all men, without regard to racial, political, social or intellectual distinctions, but in the sense that in her is to be found a place for all values, all human interests, all aspects of truth. Not without justification does she claim that, but for her, Europe would have been a wild waste of uncouth barbarism or a half-orientalised region of mingled Arabic, Slavonic and Tartar origin; but for her, the perennial thought of Greece, the poetry of Homer and Aeschylus, the eloquence of Demosthenes and Cicero, the passion of Sappho and Catullus, the soaring beauty of a thousand cathedrals would have been lost to mankind. Artistic culture is not what she treasures most. But since men treasure it so much, she is entitled to remind them that they owe some gratitude to her for its present existence.

I am well aware that, whilst much that I shall have to say will strike many of my readers as intolerably bizarre, there will be some at least who will object that what I am claiming for Roman Catholicism is the common heritage of the civilised world. Well, I should be the last to deny that Catholicism has many fellow-travellers who may not be prepared to go all the way, but who do admire much that she cherishes, who do believe much that she teaches. They are in truth Catholic in what they affirm and accept; it is in their refusals that they part company with her. The true Catholic does not pick and choose; he accepts in its entirety what he believes to be the message of Christ, with all the logical implications and inevitable developments which time has disclosed.

In a valuable book entitled *The Catholic Centre*, Mr. E. I. Watkin has developed very ably the argument that in the Roman Catholic Church alone is to be found a genuine synthesis of all that is best in different religions. "Were all religions but human guesses at truth, we should be reduced to constructing what synthesis we could of their positive doctrines. The Catholic religion however bears out its claim to be a Divine revelation of truth by the fact that its doctrinal system brings together and reconciles in its comprehensive and balanced truth the partial truths taught by all other religions, rejecting only their denials, their exclusions and their partialities. Moreover, it implies a philosophy correspondingly comprehensive and synthetic. All religions thus tend towards the Catholic religion as their fulfilment. Their divergent lines, when straightened and prolonged, meet in the Catholic centre. There the exaggerations of a partial truth, the exclusions of complementary truth, are corrected and supplied in the comprehensive truth embracing all positive religious truths. And the *via media* is maintained between all extremes. All roads lead to Rome."

'Roman Catholicism,' then, is to be taken as covering the faith and practice of those Christians who, wherever they may be found, accept the jurisdiction of that hierarchical organisation which has the bishop of Rome as its head. In an appendix we shall discuss that organisation in some detail. But since the organisation is no more than the external framework of a body which, whilst admitting the necessity for such organisation, yet believes that it is only incidental to its existence, it seems most helpful to begin with some account of what it feels like to the Catholic himself to belong to that body. He is, of course, fully aware that he belongs to an elaborately organised institution. But the chief thing that interests him is the effect that institution has on his personality and destiny. He believes indeed that certain ways of behaving are important, not in themselves, but because of the implications and effects of such conduct.

One further point must here be made. In seeking to find out what the Church stands for, we must distinguish between the essential and the accidental, between the official and the popular presentation. In matters of doctrine, only one individual, and he on rare occasions, can be taken as certainly speaking for the whole Church. There are countless individual Catholics whose utterances and whose conduct are far from representing the mind and practice of the Catholic Church. What I hope will emerge from this book is a tolerably clear picture of what Roman Catholicism means to the sincere and intelligent Roman Catholic. What it looks like from the outside is largely irrelevant. But in order to present a true picture to the onlooker, it will be necessary from time to time to suggest how, by an undue attention to the accidental and incidental, Catholicism has come to be so gravely misunderstood.

The point has been put supremely well by Maritain. "Catholics are not Catholicism. The errors, apathies, shortcomings and slumbers of Catholics do not involve Catholicism. Catholicism is not obliged to provide an alibi for the failures of Catholics. The best apologetic does not consist in justifying Catholics or in making excuses for them when they are in the wrong, but on the contrary in emphasizing their errors and in pointing out that, far from affecting the substance of Catholicism, they serve only the better to display the virtue of a religion which is still a living force in spite of them. The Church is a mystery, her head is hidden in the sky, her visibility does not adequately manifest her nature; if you seek to know what represents, without betraying, her, consider the Pope and the episcopate, teaching faith and morals, consider the saints in heaven and on earth, avert your eyes from us poor sinners. Or rather consider how the Church heals our wounds and leads us hobbling to eternal life. Leibniz pretended to justify God by showing that the work which proceeded from the hands of that perfect Workman was itself perfect, whereas in reality it is the radical imperfection of every creature which best attests the glory of the Uncreated. The great glory of the Church is to be holy with sinful members."*

CHAPTER ONE

THE FUNCTION OF THE CHURCH

THE Roman Catholic Church exists to teach men a way of life which is only incidentally related to the social or political condition of this or that epoch, and to provide men with the means to achieve a fulfilment which cannot effectively be realised in any historical situation. In other words her chief concern is with the transcendental, supernatural aspect of human experience. To understand this claim, it will be necessary to appreciate a little more exactly the meaning of the term 'supernatural'. In ordinary language, it is often used vaguely for extraordinary phenomena, psychic manifestations and the like. In Catholic theological language it has a precise technical sense, being used to specify those characteristics or activities which are not essentially related to human nature in itself. Man, as man, possesses certain 'natural' characteristics— physical, psychological, rational. He fits into the order of Nature about him. Physically, he is subject to the activities of natural forces, the law of gravity, the effects of temperature, chemical action. The sciences of biology and psychology can study and predict his reactions to appropriate stimuli. Even the activities of intellect and will fall within the sphere of philosophical analysis and explanation. Yet, inexhaustible as that study is, so that not all the findings of scientist, psychologist, poet and metaphysician succeed in stating the whole truth about "the glory, jest and riddle of the world," the Catholic believes that there is a whole world of reality to which man has been introduced, which is beyond discovery by human thought and human imagination—because it is 'super-natural'.

However whole-heartedly we may accept the theory of evolutionary development, however difficult it may be to draw the line between the different levels of actuality, we do in practice distinguish between living and non-living matter, between vegetable and animal, between brute animal and man. Now, whatever activities may be peculiar to this or that species of the class of living beings—the activities of growth and reproduction common to all forms, the activities of sensation common to man and brute, the intellectual or moral activities proper to man—all are to be ascribed to that principle of life in virtue of which alone the organism can perform them. Without necessarily demanding assent to the Aristotelian system, it may help to a clearer appreciation of this analysis if we invoke the doctrine of 'form'. According to Aristotle, then, what makes this or that living organism capable of vital activities is the 'entelechy' or 'form', the principle which so organises and vitalizes the material constituent that it is no mere sum of physical or chemical features, but behaves in ways which are beyond the capacity of the merely physical or chemical.

When we turn to discuss the meaning of the term 'super-natural', we have to try to see it in the same sort of way. The Catholic holds that there is a higher kind of vital principle, a transcendent entelechy, which renders the complicated being we call man capable of activities which are beyond his merely human capacities. As sensation and emotion are beyond the capacity of the daisy, as mathematics and musical composition, moral judgment and free choice, are outside the ken of the elephant, so is super-natural living beyond the unaided capacity of mankind. Briefly, the Catholic holds that God has chosen to elevate man to some sort of share in His own experience. And the Church claims that it is through her that God chooses to propagate this divine life.

The mere statement of such a claim must seem a piece of intolerable arrogance. Nor is the Catholic himself unaware of the stupendous assertions it involves. But there seems no other way of explaining the texts in the New Testament upon which that claim is based. "I have come so that they may have life, and have it more abundantly." (John X. 10.) "You have only to live on in me and I will live on in you. . . . If a man lives on in me and I in him, then he will yield abundant fruit. . . . The task I have appointed to you is to go out and bear fruit, fruit which will endure. . . ." (John XV. 3-16.) "Thou hast sent me into the world on thy errand, and I have sent them into the world on my errand." (John XVII. 18.) "I pray for those who are to find faith in me through their word." (John

XVII. 20.) "You therefore must go out, making disciples of all nations . . . teaching them to observe all the commandments which I have given you." (Matt. XXVIII. 19-20.)

The basis of this whole doctrine of the propagation of the divine life in the world is that truth which is central to the whole Christian tradition, the doctrine of the Incarnation. This is no place to discuss the content of that truth, which Catholic and many non-Catholic Christians alike share; but it is relevant to our task to point out that the Catholic Church has, from the first, insisted on an acceptance of the truth in its fullest and most complete form. She holds, in the first place, that, at a certain moment in history, a man was born who was, besides being wholly human, not less really divine, divine in the full sense of the word: he was God. This act by which God chose to share the human experience of the creatures he had created was a further manifestation of that incomprehensible and infinite love which not only "moves the sun and moon and other stars" but must be invoked as the only feasible explanation of God's dealings with the world. "God," in the favourite aphorism of the Greek Fathers, "became man in order that men might become gods." The reality of our supernaturalisation is proportionate to the truth of God's Incarnation. But how was this process of supernaturalisation to be achieved? Clearly, so the Catholic holds, if all men born into the world in time are to be enabled to draw near to the source of life, there must be some visible, recognizable system or institution which will make this possible. Is there such an institution and, if so, where is it to be found?

Since practically all that we know about Jesus Christ is to be derived ultimately from the New Testament records, we naturally turn to them for our knowledge of the plan and purpose of the Incarnational system. The facts about Christ's life, in broad outline, are not seriously in dispute. The tendentious and unscientific speculations of nineteenth century 'criticism' are being rapidly discredited, and as the dust of controversy settles, the traditional outlines of Christ's story are seen again with even greater clarity. And the solid factual basis of the events of his life and of the incidents outlined in the Acts of the Apostles is borne out by all that we know of contemporary

political and social history. It is certain that, after his death, a
chain of inter-connected groups of men and women came into
being in the Levant and beyond, basing the principles of their
conduct on belief in the existence of Jesus Christ and in the
reality of his continuing power. That power meant for them not
merely inspiration and instruction, but literal invigoration. He
continued his own individual existence, it was true. But, in
some profoundly actual sense, they lived by his life: he lived
on in them. Plato, Aristotle, Zeno and the rest had established
schools, in which their doctrine was handed on. But in none of
these was it claimed that the disciples derived actual vitality,
literally from the principle of life that had been present in the
founder. The Apostles claimed, indeed, to teach what Christ
had taught; but far more than that, they claimed—and their
claim was accepted—that through their hands came an actual
power, a force, by which all believers were enabled to live
transformed lives.

As time went on, these inter-connected groups, loosely
united at first in the possession of a common faith and a
common way of life, developed a stronger organic unity. The
'churches' had become the 'Catholic Church'. From the
beginning, there had been insistence on unity—the unity that
comes from mutual love, the unity that comes from faith in a
body of doctrine, the unity that comes from the possession of a
common code of moral practice. Doubtless from Judaism was
derived the notion of being a 'peculiar people', and the early
hostility both of non-Christian Jew and of pagan would help
to bind Christians together. But the unity of the Church was
something from within, fostered by men who had known the
Master, who were filled at once with passionate devotion to his
person and his ideals and with a consuming hatred for all that
might appear to be treachery to the truth as taught by him and
to the mission which he had laid upon them.

It was then from this personal knowledge and love that the
source of that early unity springs. "Where Christ is, there is the
Church Catholic," declared Ignatius of Antioch at the very
dawn of the second century A.D. Yet for all that from the
earliest times there had also been disloyalties and divisions.
St. Paul could write: "Parties there must needs be among you,

so that those who are true metal may be distinguished from the rest." (I Cor. XI. 19.) From the very beginning, therefore, the Christian Church was concerned about the problem of maintaining unity of belief. "Has Christ been divided up?" (I Cor. I. 13.) Since Christ and his truth was the sole burden of the Gospel message, it was intolerable, impossible, that a mere medley of contradictions should be all that survived of Christ's teaching in a Church that believed itself to be the vehicle and organ of his continuing life. Hence the story of St. John, fleeing in horror from the baths where the heretic Cerinthus was present. Hence the growing systematisation and organisation, beginning with the local establishments, churches with their elders, ordained by the Apostles themselves, to hand on the new life and to safeguard the faith and teaching of Christ's own commissioned teachers. "It is for thee, Timothy, to keep safe what has been entrusted to thee, avoiding these new, intruding forms of speech . . . there are those who profess them, and in professing them have shot wide of the mark which faith sets us." (I Tim. VI. 20-21.)

To the Catholic, then, it seems entirely natural to suppose that such unity could not be preserved without a teaching authority, clearly recognized and freely acknowledged. Nor, in the circumstances of the time, when all roads led to and from Rome, could any other centre for what was professedly a universal religion be more natural than the capital of the world Empire. The centre of the Christian Church was early established in Rome—how early is a matter for historians to debate—and there it has remained. That is why 'Roman' is not normally employed by Roman Catholics amongst themselves. For them it is either misleading or tautologous: misleading if it implies that there can be more than one centre of truth; if not, tautologous.

Here, of course, we are at the heart of controversy, but for our purposes, it is unnecessary to pursue the subject. Suffice it to say that the Roman Catholic is convinced that, in his insistence on the need for a centre of doctrinal authority, he is not only being faithful to the apostolic tradition but is in the line of full historical development. Believing as he does that a clear primacy was conferred on Peter in the famous words of Christ:

B

"Upon this rock I will build my Church" (Matt. XVI. 18), he finds in Gospels and Acts clear evidence that Peter's pre-eminence was accepted by his fellow Apostles, whilst the fragmentary evidence of such writings as have survived is only explicable on the supposition that by the end of the first century A.D. some special dignity attached to the Church established at Rome. Certainly in the course of the second century, doctrinal and other disputes began to be referred to the bishop of the Roman Church. The witness of Clement of Rome and Ignatius of Antioch, of Hermes and Hegesippus, of Irenaeus and Tertullian, points in the same direction. Admittedly, the evidence is scanty and, in detail, inconclusive. But the most natural explanation of such indications as we find is to be found in the view that, increasingly, the Church of Christ looked towards Rome for guidance and instruction.

It might seem to the reader that we have moved far from a discussion of the function of Roman Catholicism, with which this chapter is allegedly dealing. Yet it will be seen that a discussion of function necessarily leads on to some consideration of the nature of the functioning organism. At any rate, it is to be hoped that nothing which has been said so far will obscure the fundamental notion that what the Church exists for is the supernatural fulfilment of the human individual, that is to say, she exists to enable man to become a partaker of that divine life which, far beyond his unaided capacity, is yet offered to him by the unimaginable goodness of God. In a word, the function of the Church is the sanctification of mankind. Again, it is necessary to recall that this process of 'sanctification' is not to be conceived of in terms of some purely human self-betterment or vague moral uplift. Sanctification, as the Catholic Church conceives it, is an effect, not of human effort, though it requires human co-operation, but of divine action. But that divine action is mediated by the divinely-ordained institution, the Church of Christ, the Church founded by Christ, developed by Christ through the activities of his Apostles, the Church which remains true to itself only in so far as it remains true to Christ and his teaching, propagated by his Apostles, the Church which exists in order that all men may have the opportunity and the means to receive of the fullness of life which Christ came on earth to bring.

All this is summed up for the Roman Catholic in the statement that the true Church is One—or else Christ is 'divided up'; she is Holy—or else she has failed in her purpose; she is Catholic, in other words addressing herself to all men whatsoever—or else she has failed to listen to the command of her Founder; she is Apostolic, since it was through the teaching and activity of the Apostles that, in the course of history, she developed into a widespread visible institution.

If now we may attempt a statement of what the Roman Catholic Church is, we must try to avoid the danger of thinking of her merely as one institution amongst so many. To the non-Catholic, of course, she is just that. Harnack speaks of her in these words: "The Roman Church is the most comprehensive and the vastest, the most complicated and yet at the same time the most uniform structure which, so far as we know, history has produced." In the course of this book we shall have an opportunity of considering the structural aspects of the Catholic Church. But, at the risk of some initial obscurity, I have deliberately chosen to look at her from the inside rather than from the outside, because it is only so that we shall come to a clearer understanding of her essential nature as she herself conceives it. For the present, therefore, we must content ourselves with the statement that the Roman Catholic Church claims to be the divinely-appointed means for the continuation in time of the work of Redemption, which is the chief work of the Incarnate Word.

CHAPTER TWO

THE UNITY OF THE
ROMAN CATHOLIC CHURCH

THE key-note, then, of Catholicism is the idea of life. The Catholic regards his Church as primarily a life-giving organism, possessing in a supreme degree that which it gives. Now it is essential to any organism that it should constitute a true unity; for it is one thing, composed of parts whose activities are all directed to the common purpose of the whole. That purpose constitutes the law of its being, the law in accordance with which all the parts function. But, in so functioning, not only do the parts realise the good of the organism; through it they achieve their own fulfilment. The hand which labours to feed and clothe the body, itself profits from its activities. The eye which sees and warns of danger threatening some other part of the body, yet benefits if that other part is preserved. Unless the overriding purposes of the whole organism are kept in view, disintegration and corruption set in. The drunkard, the sensualist, the drug-addict, provide examples of the sorry effects of allowing excessive individualism to this or that instinct or tendency.

So is it with the Church. The overriding purposes for which she exists demand of her members a disciplined unity. The preservation of that unity may require of them the surrender of some immediate personal satisfaction which would, in the long run, not merely tend to the disintegration of the whole body, but would, incidentally, result in the ultimate undoing of the individual members. Hence comes about the exercise of that eternal vigilance which, here as elsewhere, is the condition of abiding liberty. Nor is this insistence on unity to be thought of as a modern invention, uncharacteristic of the great Christian tradition which Catholicism claims to uphold. In the fourth Gospel we find the need for it explicitly recognised. Christ, in his prayer for his disciples, asks his Father:

" . . . keep them true to thy name, thy gift to me, that they may be one, as we are one. . . . It is not only for them (the Apostles) that I pray; I pray for those who are to find faith in me through their word; that they may be all one. . . ." (John XVII. 11-20). And in the interesting *Shepherd* of Hermas, a second century work, we find this emphatic passage:

> "Do you not see before you a great tower, being built up with glorious squared stones? Myriads of men were bringing stones, some from the depths of the abyss, others from the earth, and they were giving them to six young men who took and built with them. The stones that were taken from the abyss were used immediately in the building; they fitted so well that no man might see where they were joined, and the whole tower looked as if it were made of a single block."
>
> (Shepherd III. ii, 4, 6.)

But there are stones which are rejected, some because they are misshapen, others because they will not stay in their place.

In other words, unity can be achieved only through a subordination of parts to the whole. True unity can persist only where there is some principle, some criterion; and those who do not accept the principle, who do not square up to the criterion, are inevitably rejected. The struggle against heresy has ever been a feature of the Christian life. It was through that struggle, as often as not, that the Church grew to appreciate more accurately the content of the truth confided to her. The work of Irenaeus at the end of the second century, *Against Heresies*, is characteristic of so much of Christian writing. It is only when you are desperately anxious about truth that you shrink from the slightest suggestion of error.

Yet it would be misleading to suggest that the Church has ever been primarily concerned with the definition of dogma for its own sake. As we have seen, her chief concern is the well-being of man in all departments, though especially in the task of safeguarding his eternal well-being. Precision of dogmatic statement is of importance because the truth about God guarantees the status of man. There is point in the Chestertonian paradox: "Doctrines had to be defined within strict limits, even in order that men might enjoy general human liberties. The Church had to be careful, if only that the world might be careless."

The Catholic, then, sees his Church progressing surely along a single line of development, safeguarding the precious heritage of revelation, constantly preoccupied with its implications, encouraging speculation that will lead to clarification, cautious in her attitude to the one-sided specialist who rides his hobby-horse to death, without reference to the general pattern of human existence. In sober fact, there has generally been something unbalanced about the men who have been condemned by the Church as heretics. Fanaticism is the mark not of orthodoxy but of error. To quote Chesterton again, "people have fallen into a foolish habit of speaking of orthodoxy as something heavy, humdrum and safe. There never was anything so perilous or so exciting as orthodoxy. It was sanity: and to be sane is more dramatic than to be mad." The orthodox man needs no fanaticism to strengthen the cause of which he is convinced.

Since truth is impatient of compromise, it has often happened that the Church has permitted whole provinces to leave her jurisdiction rather than strive to retain them by some comprehensive 'formula'. When the Gnostic sought to limit the full appreciation of the faith to an esoteric few, she defended the position of the average man against the pretensions of the pseudo-intellectual; when the Montanists and Novatians preached an intolerable ethic, again she stood for the broad humanity of a moral system which, uncompromising in its demands, yet recognized and catered for the weakness of human nature by allowing the sinner an opportunity to be restored to grace by the reception of the sacraments: when the Sabellians and Arians, Nestorians and Monophysites and the rest sought to explain the incomprehensible mysteries of the divine nature and the hypostatic union by explaining them away, she did not hesitate to condemn error, even at the risk of losing half the Empire.

There are two major examples of such division which call for special notice here. The first is the great schism by which the Eastern Church rejected the authority of the See of Rome; the second is the Reformation. If we discuss them in some detail it is because an understanding of the Church's role will help to elucidate her general attitude to the problem of unity. We have seen in brief how the central authority of Rome came to be established. It was, in a sense, an historical accident that the chief bishopric was established there. It might conceivably have remained at Jerusalem, had Jerusalem not been fore-doomed to destruction. Antioch was, for a time, of equal importance with Jerusalem; but with the spread of the Gospel westwards, the half-Oriental capital of the fallen Seleucid empire was no fit place for the head of a Church beginning to be conscious of its universal mission. Athens was now merely a provincial university. To Rome then came Peter. Ever since, the Universal Church has found its spiritual centre there.

But already in the second century the barbarian was beginning to batter at the north-eastern frontiers, and by the end of the third century Diocletian realised that the defence of the sprawling Empire could only be maintained by the division of power between East and West. Constantine completed the movement by the refounding of Byzantium under the name of Constantinople. Less than a century after that event, the capital of the western Empire was sacked by Alaric. With the establishment of the Ostrogothic kingdom in Italy and the end of the line of western emperors in 476, it looked as if the *res Romana* had reached its term. The roll of emperors begun by Augustus was interrupted in the West, but persisted in the Eastern capital. There is a sense in which the Popes of Rome, beginning with the first Gregory, assumed some of the functions of the western emperors; though Hobbes exaggerates when he describes the Papacy as "not other than the ghost of the deceased Roman Empire, sitting crowned upon the grave thereof." The Pope could still say, with his Master, "my kingdom is not of this world."

Yet we can well understand how the Patriarchs of Con-stantinople began to claim an equality of jurisdiction with the Bishops of Rome. Already in 381, at the Ecumenical Council held in the Eastern capital, it had been declared that the "bishop of Constantinople holds a pre-eminence in honour second only to that of the bishop of Rome, because Con-stantinople is the new Rome." And at Chalcedon (451), it was stated that, whilst a primacy of honour is rightly paid to the See of Rome, yet "one hundred and fifty bishops have attributed equal dignity to the most Holy See of New Rome, rightly judging that the city which is honoured with the presence of Emperor and Senate and enjoys the same rank as the elder imperial city of Rome, should in the affairs of the Church be exalted as she is, coming second after her."

Pope Leo I (440-461) refused to accept this principle. In a letter to the Emperor dated 22 May, 452, he writes: "It is our desire that the city of Constantinople possess its proper renown and under the protection of God's right hand enjoy the lasting rule of Your Clemency. But the principle by which affairs of state are judged is not that by which the things of God are decided, nor will there be any lasting edifice apart from the rock which our Lord laid as a foundation." In spite of this protest, the position of Constantinople as second to Rome was accepted and indeed incorporated in the Justinian Code.

The wisdom of Leo's protest is shown by the sequel. The presence in Constantinople of the Emperor meant, in effect, that the ecclesiastical affairs of the Eastern Church were all too frequently settled by the civil authority. Time and again we see the bishop of Rome resisting the encroachments of the emperor in theological debate. Although the secular rulers of the East continued for a long time to express their acceptance of the spiritual supremacy of Rome, they did not hesitate to assert their often heretical opinions against the decisions of the Popes. In the sixth century Pope Silverius died in exile because of a difference with Justinian, and in the following century Heraclius treated St. Martin in the same way. Between 323 and 787 there were no fewer than two hundred years during which there was widespread schism either of the entire East or at least of the regions which were under the immediate jurisdiction of Antioch and Constantinople. Once accept the fatal principle that ecclesiastical importance is to be judged by political rank, and the way is laid open to the gravest abuses. "And moreover deeper than the wounds of political vanity, deeper even, it would seem, than differences of doctrine or discipline—the insertion of the *Filioque* clause in the Creed, the use of the unleavened wafer, the celibacy of the clergy, etc.—there lay the antipathy of the two civilisations, or rather, to use the language of the Byzantines, of barbarism and civilisation. What could Constantinople have in common with the boors of the West—Constantinople, the queen of elegance, set amid the glitter of gold and precious stones on the banks of the Bosphorus?"* Yet it is a fact of history that whenever the Eastern Church rebelled against the authority of Rome, it was generally over some point of doctrine or discipline in which the verdict of Eastern and Western alike has been since given in favour of Rome. However much, at the time, Byzantium may have despised the West, the latter has been justified by history. A characteristic example is provided by the Icono-clastic controversy. During the eighth century, and especially under the Emperor Leo V (813-820), a violent onslaught was made on the practice of making and venerating images. It might seem a harmless matter, or at least one not involving any deep principle. But, as Christopher Dawson† has shown, implicit in the controversy was the whole doctrine of the Incarnation. "From the early times there has existed in the oriental border-land a type of sectarian Christianity which had nothing in common with Western orthodoxy. . . . It rejected the sacra-mental teaching of the Church and the use of external forms and ceremonies in favour of a purely spiritual and interior religious ideal. Matter was evil, and all reverence paid to material objects was essentially idolatrous. . . ." And the triumph of the image-makers proved beneficial not merely to sound theology but also to art and culture in East and West alike. It is highly significant that the leaders of the anti-Iconoclasts at Byzantium were the outstanding men of letters of the time.

But though this particular breach was healed by the initiative of the Emperor Michael II and the Empress Theodora, the seeds of future quarrels were not sterilised. At the beginning of the ninth century, St. Theodore, abbot of the monastery of Studium, at Constantinople, had written to the Emperor in these terms: "Now is the acceptable time that we should unite

* *The Life of the Church.* Ed. by M. C. D'Arcy. p. 157.
† *The Making of Europe*, pp. 180 sqq.

ourselves with Rome, the summit of the churches of God, and through her to the three other Patriarchs." Yet it was not long before an all but irrevocable step had been taken on the road to complete schism. In the year 857 the Emperor, Michael the Drunkard, and his uncle Bardas, deposed the lawful Patriarch because he had rebuked the shameless lives of the heads of the State. This man, Ignatius by name, had been duly elected by the clergy of Constantinople and his election ratified by Rome. Now, eleven years later, he was driven into exile and a remarkable man, Photius, introduced in his stead. Undoubtedly the most learned man of his generation, he might have gone down to history as one of the greatest scholars of the Byzantine world. As it is, he is chiefly remembered because of the schism associated with his name. Despite the lies and violent measures employed by the enemies of Ignatius, the Pope confirmed his appointment and refused to accept the legality of the claim put forward by Photius. Photius persisted in his usurpation and refused to acknowledge the authority of Rome. Fortunately a Palace revolution brought his tenure of office to an end. Ignatius was restored and the schism healed.

But in the 11th century the final rupture came. We cannot pursue the details of the story of Michael Cerularius who, in 1053, wantonly threw off his allegiance to Rome and took the whole Eastern Church with him in his act of rebellion. Since then, though attempts have been made to restore the situation, there has been a great gulf fixed between East and West. All that it is necessary to emphasize for our present purpose is that, invariably, the first step towards division was taken by the East, that Rome has made constant efforts to restore the situation, but that she has always refused and must always refuse to heal the breach at the price of compromise. The interests of Christ to which she believes herself divinely dedicated cannot be served by dishonesty or weakness.

The Eastern Schism, then, split the Church in two, and in the earlier stages at least it might well have seemed that Rome was allowing the wealthier and more civilised regions of Christendom to be lost for the sake of a principle. There were doubtless genuine misunderstandings on both sides and probably some failure of tact. But the story in broad outline and in detail bears incontrovertible witness to the integrity and incorruptibility of the See of Rome. Whatever accusations of personal ambition may be levelled against individual Popes, it remains certain that men like Nicholas I and Leo IX, who had to deal respectively with Photius and Cerularius, were possessed of a high sense of duty and honour. Their efforts for peace broke down because they met with dishonesty, ambition, violence and obstinate pride. Even Dvornik's recent study of Photius, whilst it emphasizes the complications of the problem, does not discredit the essential rightness of the Pope's attitude.

If we have discussed the Schism at such length it is because the story prepares us for the events of the fifteenth and sixteenth centuries, culminating in the great cleavage between Catholic and Protestant in the West. Catholic historians will be the first to admit that the story of the Church is the story of an institution which bears all the marks of its human quality as well as of its divine origin. From the earliest times there have been abuses, sometimes in the highest places in the Church. But the Catholic believes that there is an inherent power acting within the Church which prevents the worst effects of the gravest abuses. "God writes straight with crooked lines" and the Catholic believes that he is entirely justified in seeing a special Providence manifested in the history of his Church. None knows better than he what grave scandals have existed in the very highest ranks of the hierarchy: nor does he deny that ignorance and superstition, bad faith and greed, have stained the story of clergy and laity, of statesman and soldier, of every variety of Catholic in every century. For all that, he maintains that the way of reform is not to reject root and branch the whole system centred in Rome; still less to pretend that when you have done that you have somehow renewed and revitalized an organism which has flourished only in proportion to the degree in which it has maintained its coherence and its unity.

The story of the Reformation has been told so often and from so many points of view, that it must seem presumptuous to attempt to retell it in the space at our disposal. But the nature of this book requires that the attempt be made. We begin then by repeating that reformation is a permanent feature of Catholic life. St. Paul had to insist on the constant need for a rejection of unwholesome elements in the Christian communities in the very first decades of the Church's history. There was constant need for such vigilance. In the tenth century, the Cluny movement had initiated a serious attempt to deal with the appalling abuses in the ranks of the hierarchy, whilst the efforts of Hildebrand in the eleventh century and of Innocent III later show that the authorities continued the task with vigour. That there were grave abuses in the Church in the fifteenth century, no educated Catholic seeks to deny; what he does maintain is that the way of the Protestant Reformers was not for the ultimate good of Christendom. Instead of effecting an improvement from within, it introduced into the Christian body a division which has strengthened the forces of irreligion.

The unity of mediæval Christendom had been due to the recognition by the great majority of the faithful of the fact that, despite a divergence of temporal interests, the different regions of Europe had a common centre in Rome. The feudal system, produced by the wedding of features of the later Roman Empire with Teutonic institutions, had its basis in a more than local patriotism or personal loyalty. In men's minds, the notion of Rome as the eternal city was still active, so that they thought of themselves as members of a European society, a society which was the temporal reflection of the kingdom of God. Even the most ambitious and least devout emperor or king had an awe of the Pope as God's vice-gerent.

It was the new national consciousness, gradually emerging from the twelfth century onwards, which inflicted the first blow on this consciousness of an overriding unity. The Avignon interlude, when for more than a generation the Papacy fell under the control of the rising power of France, intensified the intrusion of national prejudice into men's attitude towards the See of Rome, though it has to be admitted that the Pope's position as a temporal sovereign made it difficult for men always to see the Vicar of Christ in the ruler of the Papal States.

Another important disintegrating factor was the decline in men's respect for the Church's intellectual standards. The universities, which had been founded under her auspices and had contributed to the formation of the great Scholastic synthesis, were becoming parochially minded, and the arid debates of lesser intellects invited the contempt of a new race of scholars. The learning of ancient Greece, becoming increasingly available from the thirteenth century onwards, and the invention of printing, ushered in a new outlook. That the Church was not incapable of adjusting herself to the new situation is clear from the fact that, whilst learning and the arts were patronised very largely by Churchmen, scholars like Thomas More and Pico della Mirandola had no difficulty in combining piety with erudition. But a new spirit was undoubtedly abroad, and before complete assimilation was achieved, the break had come.

The immediate occasion, Luther's attack on the abuse of Indulgences and later on various points of doctrine, might have had no very far-reaching effects had it not been for the political situation. When, a little later, the French king was fighting for the hegemony of Europe with the Emperor, he was prepared to find allies in the German princes who, for one reason or another had come to accept Protestantism, and were in opposition to the Hapsburg. This meant, in effect, that the eldest daughter of the Church was fighting side by side with the Church's enemies.

Into the tangled story which ends with the treaty of West-phalia in 1648 it is impossible to enter here, nor can we do more than allude to the bitter wars that divided France against herself and plunged Europe into the worst savageries she had known since the coming of the barbarian a thousand years before. But the general pattern is the same, doctrinal con-troversy turning political division into a war of religion; national ambition seizing on religious differences as the occasion for dividing enemies or furnishing allies; repressive measures engendering obstinacy, obstinacy exacerbating persecutors on both sides. The upshot is that, with the end of the Thirty Years' War, the great cleavage was finally established. It has never been healed. It was tragic for the Church; but in all sincerity the Church believes that it has been immeasurably more tragic for Europe. She has, after all, had a long experience of schism and heresy; she believes that she still possesses the truth, a truth clarified and vivified even further by these melancholy events. But she holds that despite all the material progress of the last two hundred years, there is a sickness in men's hearts and men's consciences which has produced the horrors of our present age.

This, then, is the Catholic attitude to the Reformation. The Church regards the work of the Reformers from Luther onwards as constituting the greatest possible disservice to the cause of Christ, which her opponents no less than she claim to have so much at heart. That there was justification for the criticisms of Luther she does not deny. But there had been much greater abuses in the Church in earlier centuries, which Popes like Hildebrand and Boniface and saints like Bernard of Cluny and Catherine of Siena had denounced and fought with no less vigour than he. You may, and indeed must, denounce the conduct of the Vicar of Christ if he prove unfaithful to his high charge. But if you deny that Christ has a Vicar on earth, you are falsifying fifteen hundred years of Christian history. That, in effect, is what the Reformation did.

Let us, however, examine a little more closely what this attitude implies. It does not imply that Catholics as a body are committed to the view that the Reformers were consciously attacking a divine institution; nor that the Church has not profited indirectly by the challenge thus thrown at her. Amongst other such indirect benefits must be numbered the summoning of the Council of Trent, with all the theological and disciplinary developments for which it was responsible. But, whatever the personal sincerity of those who initiated and supported the Protestant Reformation, the lesson of history seems to be that the religious movements outside the Church have not contributed to the well-being of Christendom any good commensurate with the injury inflicted by the secession from the historic Church of such large tracts of European territory.

At this point it seems desirable to make some statement on the Catholic attitude towards members of other communions. It will be convenient to discuss the question with reference to the familiar formula, *extra Ecclesiam nulla salus*—"out of the Church there is no salvation." Again it will be necessary to refer to the historical line of development. In the concluding passage of St. Mark's gospel occur the words: "Go out over the world, and preach the gospel to the whole of creation; he who believes and is baptized will be saved; he who refuses belief will be condemned" (Mark XVI. 15, 16.). The very entry of Christ into the world constitutes a challenge and demands a choice. He was to be "a sign which men will refuse to recognize" (Luke II. 34.). He came to bring men to a decision (John IX. 39.). Men must be either for or against: there was no middle way (Matt. XII. 30.). Whether we like it or not, therefore, the choice is presented to us; and on our decision depend eternal consequences (Matt. XI. 20 sqq.).

It follows that, if the Church is to uphold her Master's teaching, she too must present men with a choice; and the consequences of their decision are no less momentous. But of course the choice can only be given where men are conscious of the issues involved. The phrase *extra Ecclesiam nulla salus* means in effect that, since faith in the Church is the divinely instituted means of salvation, deliberate rejection of that faith involves rejection of the means of salvation, with all that that implies. The phrase does not mean that ignorance of the faith means eternal damnation, since that can only be incurred by some conscious and deliberate choice. In a famous Allocution (9 December, 1854), Pius IX thus stated the position:

"It is of faith that no man can be saved outside the Apostolic Church of Rome, that this is the one ark of salvation and that anyone who does not board it will perish in the flood; but it is to be held as equally certain that those who are in a state of ignorance about the true religion, provided the ignorance be invincible, are not held in any way blameworthy in this matter in God's eyes. Now who would take it upon himself to assign the limits of such ignorance in view of the manifold characteristics of race, geographical situation, ability and other countless considerations? When we have been freed from these bonds of flesh and see God as he is, we shall surely appreciate the close yet lovely bond that links God's mercy with his justice; but so long as we are on earth, burdened by this mortal mass which dulls the soul, let us hold most surely, in accordance with the Catholic teaching, that there is one Lord, one faith, one baptism (Eph. IV. 5); to go further in our enquiry is wicked."

That the formula has been interpreted with extreme rigidity by not a few individuals in the course of the Church's history is no doubt true; but we can allow the Pope to express the official view of the Church. The brevity and terseness of the formula is no more a sign of inhuman harshness than is the abrupt and uncompromising nature of some of the utterances of Christ himself.

So too in the vexed question of religious toleration. It must always be borne in mind that what the Church is aiming at, in so far as she is being faithful to the mission entrusted to her, is the salvation and sanctification of all men. She is bound to love all men; she is bound to do all she can to bring all men to the knowledge of the truth; her commission is not limited. From this it follows that, as far as possible, she will have in mind, in all her decisions and activities, the common good of the whole world. But as we know, in any given situation, it is necessary to limit one's objective if efficient action is to be forthcoming. Even Christ himself said things which, at the time, must have seemed intolerant to the point of brutality. "It is not right to take the children's bread and throw it to the dogs." (Mark VII. 27.) "If he will not listen even to the Church, then count him all one with the heathen and the publican." (Matt. XVIII. 17.) Yet we know that the charity of Christ embraced the whole world and that the effects of his death are not confined to any group or class or nation. "In him there is now neither Jew nor Gentile, neither slave nor free man." (Gal. III. 28.) In other words, in estimating the worth and meaning of Christ's teaching, it is necessary to see the whole scope and trend of his words and deeds, and not single out this or that item and build a theory upon that. So in judging the Church which claims to represent his mind, it is not sufficient to single out this or that declaration, or concentrate on a number of incidents in her history. This is all the more necessary when we reflect that, whilst the Church believes herself to be preserved from fundamental error or irretrievable ruin by the abiding assistance of her Founder, she does not claim to be inspired in all details by an infinity of wisdom. To a large extent she is left to work out her own destiny subject always to the overruling direction of the Holy Spirit in major decisions.

That being premised, what are the principles according to which the Church seeks to act in this matter of toleration? First of all, she believes that it is her special duty to safeguard the spiritual interests of her own children. Just as, in the struggle for existence, a parent is expected to look after his wife and family first and is not accused of selfishness in putting their interests before those of others, so, where it comes to a choice, the rulers of the Church will naturally consider how any given situation or decision is likely to affect the Catholic body. And if she believes that what is supremely precious to her, the eternal welfare of Catholics, is being jeopardised, she will fight as energetically as any earthly mother would.

But she is equally aware that the interests of her flock are, in the end, bound up with the interests of the whole world. For it is through the truth that all men find freedom. And it is as the champion of truth and freedom that the Church has always sought to conduct herself. Now that, of course, sounds like a mere whimsical paradox to those who think that enlightenment and true liberty can come only by completely unguided speculation and undisciplined 'freedom of action'. Yet untrammelled speculation and uncontrolled individualism lead in the end to confusion and anarchy. It is not an invention of Catholic theology but a sober fact of experience that the truest wisdom and the truest freedom is attained only under authority. It was the ancient Greek who taught that unlimited democracy leads straight to tyranny. Abuses of power there have, of course, frequently been in the history of the Church; but an unprejudiced reading of history surely bears out her claim that, despite abuse, civilisation has flourished best where there has been a due regard to a central authority.

Here we may usefully consider the question of liberty of conscience in its different aspects. First of all, is the Catholic allowed to think for himself, or must he surrender all private judgment and critical sense? The answer to that, quite simply and honestly, is that the only limits which are imposed on a Catholic's freedom of judgment and criticism are those which are imposed anywhere by common sense and the general needs

of society. That is to say, if I am convinced that certain things
are true, then that very fact prevents me from speculating about
the possibility of their opposites being true. I may, as a purely
speculative exercise, indulge in enquiries about the possibility
of the truth of the contradictories of the propositions of which
I am convinced—the *Summa Theologica* of St. Thomas is full
of such enquiries—but it is a sign not of intelligence but of
intellectual neurasthenia to keep an open mind about every-
thing. The Catholic, who has been convinced by the
collaboration of grace and reason that certain propositions are
incontestably true, feels no more sense of being strait-jacketed
by such conviction than does the mathematician in face of the
binomial theorem. If a fellow mathematician tried to interest
the latter in a book which set out to disprove the binomial
theorem, he would probably feel mildly impatient and regard
it as a waste of time to listen.

What he would almost certainly not do would be to allow
his colleague to teach any pupils in whose mathematical
welfare he was himself interested. Which, of course, is what the
Church does when she forbids her children to read certain
books without official sanction. Apart from saving an enormous
amount of time, this particular ruling prevents very serious
spiritual and moral calamities. To take an example from the
sphere of biblical criticism alone, how many respectable
scholars today can deny that a vast amount of time has been
wasted and an incalculable amount of spiritual harm inflicted
on half-educated minds by the irresponsible and destructive
criticism of most of the nineteenth and early twentieth century
biblical work? When the Church was being decried as timid
and obscurantist, she was, as events have proved, defending
positions to which the better scholarship is returning.
Admittedly there have been times when Catholic scholarship
has lagged behind. But after all scholars constitute a very small
fraction of the human race. And though the Church is
interested in the eternal welfare of scholars no less than in
that of her less well educated subjects, she knows that on
balance far less harm is done by excess of caution than by
indiscriminate publication of 'advanced' views. She has a duty
to truth. What the scholar does not always realise is that harm

may come to truth through a one-sided presentation of facts more easily than through a conservatism which will wait until the relevance of new facts to the general picture is more fully appreciated.

This much needs to be said. The Church has never shown herself opposed to research and investigation. What she has insisted on is that there shall be no premature publication of new theories where there is real danger that minds incapable of appreciating their tentative nature may be disturbed in their faith. Here again she is but imitating the conduct of her divine Master who himself practised an economy of revelation, adapting his teaching to the capacity of his listeners. "I have still much to say to you, but it is beyond your reach as yet."

In principle, clearly, the theory of the Index is sound. In practice it may be possible to find fault with its application to particular cases. As we have already seen, the Catholic does not pretend that the actions of authority are invariably free from error. But he knows that the wisdom of the Church is generally borne out by the course of events, and he is prepared to admit that his experience and judgment are far more limited than those of his superiors. He knows too that, where there is a solid reason for reading books that are 'forbidden' he will have no difficulty in obtaining the necessary permission. If to the non-Catholic that looks like an unwarrantable interference with the freedom of thought of an intelligent being, he can only reply in all sincerity that it seems a small price to pay for the high privilege of belonging to the Church. Quite frankly, when he recalls how Infinite Wisdom went to school at the feet of human beings, he cannot but feel it as unpardonable arrogance on his part to have any sort of resentment at all.

But what of the Inquisition? Do Catholics try to defend the savageries of the medieval heresy-hunters who tried to compel recantation by torture or condemned Jews and others to the stake? On the whole, no; though there can be little doubt now that the savageries of the Inquisition have been very much exaggerated. And if the Catholic does not defend all that the Inquisitors did, he does at least try to understand. Once again, it is the problem of principle and practice. In principle, clearly, any society has a right to defend itself against disruptive forces; clearly, too, sheer charity will demand that you make every effort to protect your neighbour from the consequences of his ignorance or wrong-headedness. Now heresy is a force that will most certainly disrupt a Christian society, since this is based on the acceptance of Christ's truth; whilst the heretic, unless persuaded to see the error of his ways, is not only a menace to other men in this world; he is an even greater menace to himself in the next. In a less sophisticated and humane age, it may well have seemed that the only way with heretics, for the sake of society and for the heretic, was to bring pressure to bear on him to recant. But undoubtedly other motives crept in, and, even allowing for exaggeration, some of the acts of the Inquisitors and of the supporting 'secular arm' seem unpardonable. Even tactically and psychologically they were mistaken and probably defeated their own ends.

But the general question of tolerance still remains. What is the official Catholic attitude to those whom she believes to be in error, whom she calls heretics? The answer to that is, that whilst the Church cannot be true to herself and her mission and at the same time compromise with falsehood, she is nevertheless officially committed to the view that the conscience of the heretic must be respected. For it is a part of her moral teaching that the individual is bound to follow his conscience even where that conscience is at fault. She may seek to correct his error, to instruct him out of it, to persuade him to renounce it; but so long as he is genuinely convinced of the truth of his position, she is bound to concede him the right to follow his own conscience. That is the clear and unmistakable view of the Church, not to be set aside or denied, whatever be the conduct of individuals or groups here or there.

✝ A word finally about the unco-operativeness of the Church. It is a constant source of irritation to non-Catholics that she should show herself so unwilling to join with members of other Christian bodies in common acts of prayer or other forms of worship. Does it not show a lack of the true spirit of Christ to be thus aloof? Well, let us try to see what sort of principles are involved. As we have seen, in the nature of the case, truth of dogmatic statement is essential to the Church's existence. From the beginning she believed that, unless she upheld in its integrity the truth committed to her, she would lose the basis of unity and of effective action. "The truth shall make you free." Clearly, then, she has to delimit very carefully the content of the truth which she believes it is her God-given duty to safeguard. All who accept that body of doctrine she welcomes to her fold; those who, for whatever reason, reject it, in whole or in part, she must exclude from her communion. She does not condemn individual consciences—let that be clear; she does condemn what she holds to be error. Obviously she cannot be consistent and, whilst saying, "This is the true religion," agree to unite with others in a *religious* act. She will co-operate with them in any kind of activity that is not specifically religious; she will co-operate on a Christian basis, that is to say, accepting the fact that they have in common with her some portion of the Christian truth. Further than that she cannot go by the very facts of the situation. Just as the Christian cannot allow himself to unite with non-Christians in any specifically religious act—since religion means such different things for either side—so does the Church feel that common *religious* activity is impossible for Catholics and non-Catholics.

CHAPTER THREE

THE THEOLOGY OF ROMAN CATHOLICISM

I

HISTORICAL DEVELOPMENT

ROMAN Catholic theology is an immense subject. The Roman Catholic holds that the Christian revelation, essentially contained in the writings of the New Testament, has become progressively clearer and its formulation more adequate and precise, under the action of the Holy Spirit, working through many secondary causes right down to the present day. It begins with the Sermon on the Mount. In a sense it begins with the Pentateuch, because the whole Jewish tradition, contained in the books of the Old Testament, went to the fashioning of Christ's human knowledge and is therefore implicit in his utterances and in those of the Jewish Apostles. But, just as much that was implicit in the writings of the Old Testament was not understood until, in the fullness of time, the Law and the Prophets were fulfilled, so is there much in the words of Christ and in the writings of Peter and John, Paul and James, which the succeeding centuries have learnt to appreciate with increasing exactness. "I have still much to say to you," said Christ to His Apostles, "but it is beyond your reach as yet. It will be for him, the truth-giving Spirit, when he comes, to guide you into all truth . . . He will make plain to you what is still to come." (John 16, 12-13.) "Behold I am with you all the days that are coming, until the consummation of the world." (Matt. 28, 20.)

We begin, then, with a discussion of the Catholic attitude to the writings of Scripture, as the vehicle of God's revelation of His truth. Old and New Testament alike she holds to be divinely inspired, in the sense that the ultimate author is the Holy Spirit, employing human agencies. The revelation which begins with the Book of Genesis ends with the Apocalypse of

St. John. For with the closing of the New Testament writings she declares that the essentials of God's message to the world were completed. In the technical phrase, the 'deposit of faith' entrusted to her was 'closed'.

Yet the understanding of that message is something which requires the operation of many minds, scrutinising and handing on their views of the content of the deposit. Hence, side by side with the authority of Scripture, the Church has always appealed to the authority of Tradition. Before the New Testament was begun, she was already in existence, teaching and sanctifying, and however great her reverence for the letter of the scriptural statement, she maintains that the interpretation of that letter is not something to be left to the whim of the private individual, but must be controlled by the living authority through which the Holy Spirit continues His work in the world. There is indeed much in Catholic theology which is not explicitly formulated in the books of the Bible. Yet the Church maintains that the same thought is expressed because the same voice and the same mind produce the later statements, which are to be regarded as expansions of the primitive utterance. She claims that Catholic theology in its latest and fullest development is as recognisably the same organic entity as the primitive deposit, even as the full-grown man is recognisably one with the infant.

We may define theology, in its present context, as the body of statements constituting the subject-matter of the Roman Catholic faith. Within that body a distinction is to be drawn between statements which are strictly 'of faith' (*de fide*) about which, so to say, the Church has made up her mind, and others which have not been formally defined, or accepted without formal definition, though even amongst these there will be found some about which the opinion of the experts is so unanimous as to constitute a quasi-official opinion. The Catholic holds that the sum of Christian truth is possessed by him in its entirety, whilst the precise formulation of it is necessarily inadequate and incomplete. At first sight this may seem to be self-contradictory; but it is characteristic of all human thought. As Newman put it:

"If Christianity is a fact, and impresses an idea of itself
on our minds and is a subject-matter of exercises of the
reason, that idea will in course of time expand into a multitude
of ideas, connected and harmonious with one another, and
in themselves determinate and immutable, as is the objective
fact itself which is thus represented. It is a characteristic of
our minds, that they cannot take an object in which is sub-
mitted to them simply and integrally. We conceive by means
of definition or description; whole objects do not create in
the intellect whole ideas, but are, to use a mathematical
phrase, thrown into series, into a number of statements,
strengthening, interpreting, correcting each other, and with
more or less exactness approximating, as they accumulate,
to a perfect image . . . And the more claim an idea has to
be considered living, the more various will be its aspects."

(Development of Doctrine, p. 55.)

If then I hold that Christ's teaching is to be accepted in its
entirety, I shall inevitably accept every logical implication of
that teaching. And the history of Catholic theology is the story
of the study of those logical implications. Paul, with his tremendous appeals to the early Christians, Peter with his simpler
yet not less profound insistence on the demands of the Christian
life, John with his almost childlike naivety, whether in his
reiterated "Love one another" or the primitive yet penetrating
imagery of the Apocalypse, are all contributing to the building
up of a theology. Irenaeus and the Alexandrian Clement,
Tertullian, Origen and Cyprian, local provincial synods or
councils, these too added their share. With the emergence of
the Christian Church from the Catacombs in the reign of
Constantine, began the series of great Ecumenical Councils at
which the whole body of Bishops, with the Roman Bishop at
their head, wrestled with the task of fixing in the mould of
human language the fluid and subtle truths by which they
lived. They have been sneered at by the sceptic for quarrelling
about a vowel. But if you are dealing with eternal truth, the
greatest precision of statement is demanded. Side by side with
the defining Councils—Nicaea, Constantinople, Ephesus,
Chalcedon—went the speculative activity of the Greek Fathers.
But gradually the balance was shifting westwards.

It was Augustine who at once determined that the future of Catholic theology was to be with the West and himself made the greatest personal contribution to its formulation. His monumental work on the Trinity, his writings on Scripture, his astonishing correspondence, his sermons, above all his refutation of Pelagianism and his formulation of a doctrine of Grace set upon Catholic theology an ineffaceable stamp. Although, with the breakdown of the Roman Imperial power in the provinces west of the Danube and the Nile, it might seem that the centre of Christianity would return to the East, the truth is that, whilst to a large extent the Christian life stagnated in the Byzantine lands, it took on a fresh vitality from the converted Teutons in the lands of Gaul, Britain and Spain. That achievement was due, under God, to the energy of the Bishops of Rome and the untiring labours of the monks of the West. Little enough was done for centuries to advance the cause of theological learning. The great thing was that it survived.

With the revival of learning and the establishment of the Universities in the twelfth century came a recrudescence of theological activity. The pure theologian was scandalised by the 'dialectician', but a synthesis of faith and reason was achieved and in the thirteenth century we encounter the massive figure of Thomas Aquinas with his monumental system in which physics and metaphysics, scripture and logic were enlisted in the service of theology, queen of the sciences. It is no exaggeration to say that all subsequent theological speculation in the Catholic Church has been influenced, directly or indirectly, by the great Dominican.

Not that Catholic theology since his time is to be thought of as nothing more than a series of commentaries or glosses on the *Summa Theologica*. At all periods, vigorous work has been done by members of other schools and other religious orders, one of the most fruitful of such periods being in the sixteenth and seventeenth centuries when, under the double impetus of the Reformation attacks and the extremism of the Jansenists, the Society of Jesus produced a succession of competent men, chief of whom is probably Robert Bellarmine, known in this country for his controversies with James I. In the nineteenth century the most outstanding figure was Cardinal Newman, although he stands outside the ranks of the professional theologians.

II

THE CONTENT OF CATHOLIC THEOLOGY

(a) God and Creation

The centre of Catholic theology, as it is the basis of all religious activity, is the idea of God. For all her insistence on man's need of divine grace, the Church is not less concerned to assert the competence of human reason in its own sphere. And since that sphere is the world of the real and God is the most real of all beings it follows logically that man can know of his existence and something of his nature apart altogether from what he himself has revealed. So far then from belittling the part that reason plays in man's religious life, the Church is the most valiant of all its champions. For without the sound basis of rational knowledge there is no sort of guarantee that one's further speculations will not turn out to be based on illusion. On the other hand, for any lasting and profound appreciation of the nature of God, we must turn to revelation.

Here we encounter the sublime and deeply satisfying doctrine of the Holy Trinity, a doctrine that is beyond the capacity of man's reason to discover for himself, yet once revealed it comes in to satisfy the enquiring mind with the assurance that the aspirations of the human heart are not in vain. The ultimate truth, as it is known in God, is that reality contains, is, personality, intelligence, love. For this doctrine tells us that the Godhead is a society of three divine persons, knowing and loving each other so entirely that not merely can none of them exist without the other, but in some mysterious way, each is what the other is. In the deepest communion of man and woman, each desires to surrender so completely to the other as to be absorbed in that other. But it is part of the limitation of our nature that, even in the closest intimacy, this mutual surrender remains so partial and incomplete. In the Godhead, we are told, separate Persons yet possess one identical nature. So completely does the Father give himself to the Son that whatever the Father is that the Son is; so close is the bond of love uniting Father and Son that the Spirit of love proceeding from their twofold personality, whilst himself an infinitely perfect person, is all that they are. Each Person remains himself; yet there is nothing of the divine essence that is not fully shared by each.

Over against God, self-existent Being, stands the whole of created reality, dependent entirely for its existence upon the act by which God calls it out of non-existence. At one end of the scale are the angelic intelligences, approximating most closely, yet still infinitely separate from, the Intelligence that is God. At the other end is the material framework constituted no less in being by the creative act. Catholicism has always set its face against the Manichaean dualism which would find in matter something intrinsically evil, recalcitrant to the Will of God, owing its existence to an opposite principle, sheerly bad as he is sheerly good. For the Catholic, all that is at all, because it shares in the good of existence is, so to put it, on the side of God. And man, half-intelligence, half-matter, stands in the centre of the created scale. Flesh and spirit combine to form one entity, flesh the instrument and not the enemy of spirit, spirit the master but not the slave-owner of flesh. For Plato, human perfection was to be achieved by an attempt at some unnatural divorce of soul from body. But, whatever in practice may have been said by some Catholic ascetics, that is not a Catholic ideal.

And yet it is true that, in effect, there is a kind of warfare between the two, a warfare which shows that the ideal state of affairs is not the actual one. This disharmony is due to what is called by Catholic theologians Original Sin. Somewhere at the historical origin of the human race is to be found a cause for this disharmony. Never has man been at peace with himself because the most difficult of all lessons is that our peace is to be found not in doing our own will but in the will of God. Therefore, teaches the theologian, man is in this perpetual state of rebellion, of disobedience to the law of his peace. The body clearly tends to go its own way, heedless of the higher claims of the spirit. The story of the human race is a story of failure after failure, due to the invitation to put bodily comfort, bodily satisfactions, bodily pleasures before the summons of duty or the call of nobility.

Video meliora proboque
Deteriora sequor

is the confession of almost every member of the human race.

(b) Incarnation and Redemption

It is at this point that we approach the specific truth of the Christian faith, the doctrine which separates it off from all other forms of religious belief, the doctrine of the Incarnation. We have already referred to it in discussing the function of Catholicism; now we can see its place in the general pattern of Catholic belief. If we accept the view that God is completely sufficient of Himself, being the source of all that is, then we cannot explain the fact of his creating at all, except on the supposition that his very goodness involves the absolute unselfishness that love is. Loving then with complete un-self-regardingness means having an object to love. In the absence of such an object, how natural to suppose that love creates beings to love, beings whose prime purpose is to be objects of love. Not less natural is it to suppose that, having created, God might well wish to institute some real fellowship with his creation.

Whatever we may think of such speculations, the Catholic holds it for an incontrovertible fact that God did, as a matter of history, enter into a special union with his creation when he became man. Some of the loveliest legends of paganism had envisaged dimly precisely such a condescension. It was left to Christianity, once again, to assure men that there was validity in their aspirations and dreams. Within the Catholic tradition there are two schools of thought. On one side, the opinion of the great Franciscan doctor, Duns Scotus, is that the Incarnation was, so to say, the logical outcome of creation. The other, with the great name of Thomas Aquinas to commend it, teaches that the purpose of the Incarnation was remedial and redemptive, that it was, in a sense, conditional on man's fall from grace. Man had been created in a state of integrity, of friendship and communion with God; by his rebellion he had forfeited that favoured state, and of himself was unable to restore the situation. It was restored by God himself, the Second Person of the Blessed Trinity taking a human nature, and in that human nature living out to the full the possibilities of manhood. Man sinned by seeking to make himself a law unto himself, reversing the natural order. "Sin," as Augustine tells us, "is the love of the creature going as far as contempt of God." Christ restored the balance. For him, the claims of the Father were paramount. Nothing but the entire fulfilment of the divine will was to be the law of his life. In the pursuit of that ideal he incurred the hostility and hatred of those who sought to find satisfaction in some sort of compromise—hypocrisy, time-serving, selfishness, cruelty, lack of sympathy with human suffering, greed, ostentation, pride, lust. All these he condemned, not merely by his words but still more by what he did and by what he was.

The result was Calvary. Dying as he did, the innocent victim of hatred and weakness, he triumphed over weakness and hatred. In him mankind rose to its sublimest heights; and, because he was not merely man, the sublime human achievement was taken up into the very life of God. In him mankind was transfigured, redeemed. Once again we remind ourselves that whatever man does he does only in the power of God. So the Catholic doctrine of Redemption insists that this work of restoration is no mere human achievement—that would be impossible, since no human satisfaction can repair an outrage to divine justice. The scale of the sin must be repeated in the scale of the atonement. And so, in a sort of lyrical frenzy, the Church sings on Easter Eve: *O felix culpa, quae talem ac tantum meruit habere redemptorem.* "Happy sin, deserving a redeemer of such a quality!"

(c) The Mass and the Sacraments

But that is not the end of the story; in a sense it is only the beginning. For if mankind be redeemed and restored to friendship with God, that redemption can only become effective where the individual gives his assent. God does not save man against his will. That is why, as the Catholic holds, Christ instituted the whole sacramental system and the Church by which the sacraments were to be administered. Christ redeemed mankind by living a human life—by action. What he did, of course, was of value only in so far as it represented a willing and eager readiness to do always what he knew to be right in the eyes of God. So is it with all human acts. The lover's kiss, the subject's obeisance, the gesture of sympathy—these are valued not in themselves but as manifesting an inner attitude. They are appropriate to express that attitude; they can be divorced from it, but so divorced they lose their true value. So, analogously, with the sacraments of Christ's Church. Seven in number—Baptism, Confirmation, Holy Eucharist, Penance, Extreme Unction, Holy Order, Matrimony—they express in outward symbol some inner reality that is being brought about.

The core and centre of the whole sacramental system is the Holy Eucharist. It calls for extended treatment because, whilst it is, in its full development, the doctrine which is most peculiarly Catholic, it is probably the one which is least understood outside the Church. It was, of course, one of the earliest occasions of misunderstanding, for it undoubtedly gave rise to the accusation of cannibalism which was flung at the Christians in the first century of their existence; in its developed form it was the occasion of some of the bitterest controversies of the sixteenth and seventeenth centuries. Nor is it merely a matter of dogmatic belief; it also enters most intimately into the devotional practice of the members of the Church.

What then does the doctrine involve? Believing as he does that Christ is the Incarnate God, the Catholic is prepared to accept at their face value the otherwise incredible words: "This is my body." That the words were uttered by Truth itself is a part of his faith; that faith enables him to accept their plain sense. All the objections of students of Comparative Religion do not, of course, in any way invalidate that meaning. The Catholic is not deficient in common sense and if he finds in pre-Christian rites hints of a god slain and eaten, it is entirely natural to him to suppose that we have here evidence of a deep-seated desire on the part of human nature to come into the closest possible relationship with the object of religious worship. It is entirely in keeping, then, that that desire should have been so remarkably satisfied. What the student of Comparative Religion has rarely the time to study is the profound theological implications of the Catholic doctrine.

We have spoken much already of that life which Christ brought into the world, which the Church exists to propagate. It is precisely through this sacrament of the Bread of Life that that propagation is achieved. Ordinary life is supported by food; wheat is the 'staff of life'. If some divine gesture were to be made which would communicate to mankind this supernatural life, how could it be expressed more suitably than by such 'supersubstantial bread', possessing all the appearances of everyday bread, yet charged with this supernatural efficacy because it is indeed the body of God made man. That body, for all its human quality, is yet, because of the Hypostatic Union—the union in one Person (*hypostasis*) of two natures—a body in which flows the divine life itself. And, since apparent bread is that body, the poet's words express a profound truth:

"Low-latched in leaf-light housel his too huge godhead" words that recall an even greater poet's line:

"Unhousel'd, disappointed, unanealed."

Our own Shakespeare shows himself in the full Catholic tradition of sacramental faith and practice. In accepting the doctrine of the Real Presence, the doctrine that God himself is literally there in the consecrated wafer, the Catholic knows himself to be in the full tradition that goes back beyond Shakespeare and the Reformation, to the great eucharistic hymns of that towering genius, Thomas Aquinas; back to Hildebrand and the condemnation of Berengarius; back to the Catacombs and their drawings; back to the Christians of Bithynia, examined on this very matter by the Roman proconsul, Pliny; back to Ignatius, martyred under Trajan, seeing in the Eucharist at once a symbol and a guarantee of unity; back to the teaching of Paul to the Corinthians. Even before the days of Christ, he believes that the prophet Malachy foretold this mystery, and in the almost legendary figure of Melchisedech, offering bread and wine, he sees one who foreshadowed the full truth.

Those who read with sympathy and understanding the poem of Gerard Manley Hopkins, *The Bugler's First Communion*, will have some insight into what the Catholic feels about the moral effects of

Christ's royal ration

as the priest-poet prays for the young soldier that his 'kind comrade' may

Dress his days to a dexterous and starlight order.

But the effects are deeper still; for by this communion the Catholic believes that he is caught right up into the divine order.

The mystery is of course incapable of full analysis or explanation; but this much may be said: In common with the vast majority of his fellow-Christians, the Catholic believes that on Calvary a unique event occurred. Crucifixion was far commoner in those days than is hanging today. But the crucifixion that occurred on that April morning in the year 33 A.D. had a unique quality about it. Externally, doubtless, in its brutality and horror it was much like any other such execution. But the mere externals of that death—the torture of that racked body, the oozing blood, the thirst and loneliness and squalor—were no more than the visible trappings of an invisible victory, the triumph of a human will over human weakness. "No man takes my life from me; I lay it down of my own accord." (John 10: 18.) In those moments was manifested to the full the resolute purpose of a man who never swerved from the path of duty. Because he was what he was, this hideous death was imposed on him by his enemies; because he was what he was, he accepted it freely. Thereby human nature was re-ennobled in him; mankind was redeemed. It was redeemed not by the sufferings as such, the blood shedding as such, the death as such; it was redeemed by the act of will which clothed itself in these visible forms. *Non mors sed voluntas placuit sponte morientis* as St. Bernard says: "it was not his death but the will that freely embraced death which won God's pleasure." What counted, in the end, was not what Christ did or suffered but what he was. What he was the Father knew by his vision of his Son's human will; we know it only by knowing what it involved. God, for instance, knows the courage in the heart of a man, whether or not he performs deeds of bravery; we only know it when it is put to the test, when he remains faithful under stress, when he does something brave.

In other words what we call the sacrifice of Calvary is, in the final analysis, the sacrificial attitude of will, manifesting itself outwardly in concrete incident. And the Church's doctrine of the Mass supposes the view that the sacrifice of Calvary, the sacrificial state of Christ's human will, is an abiding reality, one and indivisible, the unique sacrifice of our redemption. For, in or out of time, there is no failure in that complete subordination of human will to divine will which is the expression of human perfection. But that abiding, invisible reality, is made visible in time and space to us human beings, who like to see things happening. What happened on Calvary was the original manifestation to men of the sacrifice of Christ; what happens daily in the Mass is, on the Church's view, a new manifestation each time of the same abiding sacrifice. Far then from the doctrine of the Mass derogating from the dignity of Calvary, as some of the Reformers declared, it fulfils and enhances it. Christ is not slain by the hands of the priest, as he was slain by the Jews; no such horror is suggested by the Church. Christ died once and dies no more. Only, the sacrifice which was once shown forth in his death is now shown forth daily in the liturgical act which represents afresh, makes present over and over again, in a different yet equally visible form, the one invisible and indivisible reality.

But there is more than a mere reminder of his death; the Catholic, in assisting at Mass, associates himself in will and intention, with that death. The victim of Calvary is really present on the altar; the Christian is summoned to become a fellow-victim. It is precisely through this co-operative activity on the part of the members of the Church that Christ's redemptive work is prolonged in time. The immense store of supernatural power accumulated by Christ is, so to speak, tapped by the activities of Christ's followers; they do not create or add to that store; but, by God's decree, it is through their secondary instrumentality that the power is distributed.

It will be seen then that the Catholic teaching on the Mass is no invitation to a placid and peaceful surrender; it is a summons to energetic activity. In the Mass the believer draws close to the source of power that, being himself empowered, he may go out and energize others: in Holy Communion, he literally receives that Source of Power.

It is not without reason, then, that at the very heart of Catholic devotional practice has always been the Mass. And it is because she has such a sense of the tremendous value and richness of this liturgical act that the Church has so consistently required of her children attendance at it. When, as so often happens, the cry goes up that the churches are empty on Sunday mornings, an exception must always be made of Catholic churches where, Sunday after Sunday, because of the Church's law, congregations will be found filling even the largest buildings. It is possible to criticize the law, to speak of 'mechanical attendance' and 'meaningless ritual'. Nor do we suggest that Catholics have an adequate appreciation of what they are about in 'hearing Mass'. But who can doubt that the tonic effect of even compulsory attendance is far preferable to the heedlessness of those who are not so compelled? And who is to estimate the influence of such great corporate acts of worship?

Having dwelt at such length on the central Sacrament—which is so much more than a mere Sacrament—we can deal more rapidly with the remaining six. The first and basic one is, of course, the sacrament by which in a symbolic washing, the child (or adult convert) is baptized into the life-giving Church of Christ. Here the command of Christ is so explicit that there is a universal acceptance amongst Christians of all denominations of the need for this sign of adhesion to Christ. It may be worth mentioning the passage in St. Paul's epistle to the Romans, in which, drawing his imagery from the ancient ritual in which the neophyte went down into a pool for the ceremony, he reminds his readers: "In our baptism we have been buried with him, died like him, that so, just as Christ was raised up by his Father's power from the dead, we too might live and move in a new kind of existence." Once more, we see the motif of life, a new sort of life. Christ died and rose again: the Christian dies to sin, so that he may rise again in a supernatural existence.

The remaining sacraments have a more precise application. Confirmation, in which the candidate is symbolically anointed with oil, as the athlete of old rubbed his body with oil as a preparation for the contest of the arena, is intended to strengthen the young Christian as he embarks on the battle of life; Matrimony, in which the partners solemnly pledge eternal fidelity, brings with it the special graces required in the married state; the last anointing, Extreme Unction, recalls the passage in St. James' epistle: "Is one of you sick? Let him send for the presbyters of the Church, and let them pray over him, anointing him with oil in the Lord's name. Prayer offered in faith will restore the sick man, and the Lord will give him relief" (5 : 14, 15); whilst Holy Order is the sacrament in which the ministers of God's grace are ordained, as the Apostles ordained their successors, by the laying on of hands, and other symbolic acts.

The Sacrament of Penance calls for a more special mention. The Church takes seriously the words of Christ: "When you forgive men's sins, they are forgiven, when you hold them bound they are held bound." (John 20 : 23.) And again she may be pardoned for having taken them seriously and for having maintained her attitude in face of hostility and bitter attack. She did so simply because she believed that it was a duty imposed on her by her Founder. The latest findings of psychologists suggest that the healing power of the confessional is not confined to the supernatural order. It may be advisable to add that the strictness with which the secrecy of the confessional is enforced by the authorities of the Church is of a degree incomparably higher than that which preserves the ordinary professional secrecy. No priest, under the most severe penalties may, in any circumstances whatsoever, divulge the sins which have been mentioned to him in Confession. There have indeed been occasions on which men have died rather than violate the 'seal' of the confessional.

To remove another common misunderstanding, it is worth while repeating that one of the conditions on which the priest absolves the penitent is that the latter shall be genuinely sorry for what he has done. The Catholic knows that if he confesses his sins without sorrow for them and with no intention of not repeating them he is not merely wasting his time but is committing an even greater sin of sacrilege. Those who have read Graham Greene's *Brighton Rock* will recall the moving passage when Rose told Pinkie of her visit to the church on her way to the registry office:

> "I wanted to be in a state of grace when I married you." She took no notice at all of Dallow. The theological term lay oddly and pedantically on her tongue. They were two Romans together in the grey street. They understood each other. . . . ". . . But then I remembered. It wasn't any good confessing. I went away." She said with a mixture of fear and pride: "We're going to do a mortal sin." The boy said with bitter and unhappy relish: "It'll be no good going to confession ever again as long as we're both alive."

But if a Catholic confesses his sins, accuses himself to the priest (who has received from God at his ordination the power to forgive sins), provided that there is in his heart genuine repentance coupled with an intention not to sin again, he holds that God's pardon descends upon him. And though some act of atonement, some 'penance' appointed by the priest, must be performed as a guarantee and token of repentance, the barrier which stood between him and God's friendship is taken away.

The work of the Redemption, the work begun on Calvary, continues down the ages, as children are baptized into the Church, sins absolved, the life-giving Body of Christ taken upon the tongue, the oil flowing in Confirmation, Holy Orders and Extreme Unction administered, marriage vows blessed by Christ to become not merely a pledge but a means of help to remain faithful to that pledge. The whole of man's career on earth is thus dedicated and raised to a new dimension of meaning and power.

(d) The Destiny of Man

For the Church holds that her chief concern is with the

eternal welfare of her children. We shall discuss elsewhere her attitude to his temporal problems. She has taken to heart the warning implied in the sombre question: "What shall it profit a man if he gain the whole world and suffer the loss of his own soul?" Death and its attendant Judgement, Hell and Heaven are the four unforgettable Last Things.

Not that death is for the Catholic the bleak destiny that made Aristotle regard it as the greatest of terrors—"because it is the end." For the pagan with his uncertain hope of immortality it could not be other than a terror.

Nox est perpetua una dormienda

is the burden of so much ancient literature. Philosophers speculated about a future life; Socrates, it would seem, had sure convictions. The message of Easter, the historical fact of Christ's own Resurrection from the dead, comes in to fulfil the aspirations of man's heart. We shall all die indeed; but beyond death lies eternal life. It is not the end but the beginning. Therefore, although there is much insistence in Catholic teaching and preaching on the fact of death, it is regarded not so much as significant in itself, but as constituting the term of this temporary stage of soul-making. What a man is at death, that he is, for good or evil, irrevocably. It is, of course, the tradition upon which so much of our English thought has been fashioned.

"To sleep; perchance to dream: ay, there's the rub . . ." The modern sentimentality which masquerades as enlightenment would suggest that the world is not a vale of soul-making, but a vale of make-believe. Whether or no there be any future beyond the grave, it makes no difference whether a man has striven for righteousness during this life or has rejected all moral standards and battened on others. Damnation is an outmoded superstition; if there is a future life, all will be well for everybody; if there is not, then why pretend that there are eternal issues involved in man's deliberate choices?

The Church holds that the teaching of Christ on the point is emphatic and unmistakable. "Come ye blessed . . . Depart from me, ye cursed . . ." That is the reason for the uncompromising stand she takes. She claims to be respecting man's dignity even as God himself respects it. Making every allowance for ignorance and stupidity and passion, she nevertheless insists that, in human choice there is an element of finality, of lasting significance. The choice can be recalled by the individual himself by an act of repentance. But it is false and ignoble to pretend that it has never been made; or if made that it does not matter. The destiny of man on this earth has been fashioned precisely through such human choices; there is no evidence to suggest that their effects may not endure into eternity.

Hell therefore is a fact. Man's evil choices, if not rescinded by himself, have their abiding result. But Heaven too is not less a fact. Heaven indeed is what man is meant to attain—a state of entire beatitude in which man's whole nature is to find the fulfilment which it does not achieve on earth. The Church's doctrine of the resurrection of the body comes in to remind us that it is man's *whole* nature which is thus fulfilled. Attempts have been made to portray the life of the blessed in heaven. All we know is summed up by St. Paul: "So we read of, things no eye has seen, no ear has heard, no human heart conceived, the welcome God has prepared for those who love him." (I Cor. 2 : 9.) Christ has told us that in heaven "there is no marrying and giving in marriage." (Matt. 22 : 30.) Sexual activity will come to an end; but the deep satisfaction of the spirit which is so dimly realised in the most perfect bodily union will be achieved in an inconceivably richer and more abiding way. The conventional representations of an endless banquet or a continuous musical performance are, of course, no more than hints at that fulfilment of the nature of man as a whole which, in this earthly existence of ours, is so often dependent on physical activity.

(e) The Blessed Virgin

No account of Catholic doctrine would be complete without some statement of the position of the Blessed Virgin in the Church, partly because of the importance of the subject in itself, but perhaps still more in a book of this kind because it is a subject which to the non-Catholic calls most urgently for explanation. We may begin by pointing out what we may describe as the logic of the situation. In the fully developed form of the Christian faith, as we have seen, the doctrine of the Incarnation holds a central position. Now, that doctrine involves a difficult intellectual feat—the maintenance of two complementary yet almost contrary truths, the existence in one being of two distinct natures—the human and the divine. In the earliest ages of the Church, with vivid memories of Christ himself or of those who had known Christ to keep alive the consciousness of his humanity, the difficulty chiefly felt was to recognise his divinity. Some indeed were so conscious of his divinity that they fell into the error of Docetism, the view that Christ only appeared to be man, his apparently human activities being a sort of make-believe; but the majority —like Browning's Karshish—would be staggered at the thought of God appearing on earth at all in human guise. During the following centuries the debate swung between the extreme of Apollinarianism, which asserted the divinity at the expense of the humanity and Arianism, stressing the humanity to the peril of the divinity. At the Council of Ephesus (431), Cyril of Alexandria's formula was formally approved: "If anyone does not acknowledge that Emmanuel is in truth God and hence that the Blessed Virgin is the Bearer of God, inasmuch as she bore in the flesh the Word of God made flesh, let him be anathema."

It will be seen then that the insistence on the dignity of Mary as Mother of God springs from a desire to maintain the full truth about the two-fold nature of her Son. It is from this position that the whole teaching and practice of the Church about the Blessed Virgin has stemmed. Whilst it may seem to many outside the Catholic tradition that local manifestations of devotion to Mary have been extravagant and unbalanced, there cannot be the slightest doubt that the official teaching of the Church about her and the general sense of the faithful have helped enormously to maintain an orthodox and balanced view of the doctrine of the Incarnation and have introduced into what might have been a mere piece of dogma a valuable element of human tenderness, bringing the whole scheme of the Incarnation into relation with everyday life of mankind. Without stressing the loss to Christian art which would befall were all Madonnas obliterated, let us mention the effect on the lives of millions of such representations as the Christmas Crib, the Holy Family, the Rood, the Pieta. Or take two items of the Catholic faith which cause so much perplexity to so many non-Catholics—the doctrine of the Immaculate Conception and that of the Virgin Birth. The doctrine of the Immaculate Conception, long held by the Church and officially 'defined' in 1854, is the counterpart of the doctrine of Original Sin, already discussed. The Catholic holds that Mary, destined to be Mother of God, was never for one instant of her existence in that state of enmity to God which is the common inheritance of mankind. This privilege of hers, making her

> Our tainted nature's solitary boast,

does not mean that she falls completely outside the economy of the Redemption. It simply states that, so closely was her life linked with that of her Son, so intimate was the link binding her with his redemptive work (so that we may say that the Incarnation could not happen until she gave her consent), that in her case a special privilege applied to her soul in the very instant of its creation a superabundance of her Son's merits. The innocent manhood he drew from her shared with her by anticipation some of its own innocence.

The doctrine of the Virgin Birth again is an indication of the high esteem in which the Church holds the Sacred Humanity of Christ. The Church, as we have seen, holds no Manichaean views about human birth; but at the same time she acknowledges the deep sense of reverence surrounding the mysterious processes of conception, and she maintains that a study of the available evidence (including, of course, the authoritative warrant of Scripture) bears out the view that the unique dignity of Mary's contribution to the life-giving work of her Son set her apart from all other human motherhood. Conceiving her Son, not through the intervention of a mortal man, but in the overshadowing of the Holy Spirit's power, she not only preserved her virginity even in that not-to-be-repeated motherhood, but she knew no ordinary conceiving or motherhood thereafter. She is at once type and inspiration to all who serve God in virginity or in motherhood, perfect and supreme in both.

CHAPTER FOUR

THE MORAL AND SOCIAL TEACHING OF CATHOLICISM

THE function of the Catholic Church, as we have seen, is the super-naturalisation of the human person. That is to say, the Catholic hopes to realise a perfection which is more than a human perfection, since it involves the elevation of his whole nature to a level at which it is capable of effecting results incommensurate with mere human powers. Such fulfilment can only be brought about by the operation of a supernatural principle, by the gift of that grace which is a divine power, introduced into human nature through the Incarnation of God himself. It is nevertheless of the first importance to remember that the raw material of this operation is precisely human nature. The perfect super-naturalisation of human nature involves, indeed implies, the perfection of human nature. It is with this aspect of the matter that we shall now be concerned.

When we turn to discuss the moral teaching of Catholicism, we find much that is common between it and the great ethical principles by which man's conduct has always, at least ideally, been governed. In certain details it is true the Church holds that Christ improved on the moral consciousness of, say, the Jews, and she believes that, in virtue of her divine commission, she has a clearer insight into the nature of human personality, bringing with it a clearer appreciation of moral principles. But it is wrong to think that the moral law as it binds Catholics is essentially different from that which binds all men. There is a widespread notion that the Church has a stricter code in sexual matters, for example, that divorce and contraception are wrong only for Catholics, although they are not wrong for those not belonging to the Church. But the Church does not believe that her commission includes the power to enlarge the scope of the moral law, though it may be true that, as in the sphere of dogma there is development, so in the sphere of ethical teaching a progressive enlightenment or increasing sensitivity to the objective demands of the moral law comes about through the activity of the Holy Spirit.

Stated simply, the Church's moral teaching declares that there is a universal moral law, binding on all men as men, inherent in human nature. It is noteworthy that St. Thomas Aquinas, in his compendium of theology, elaborates a system of ethics very largely based on the Nicomachaean Ethics of Aristotle. But the great contribution which the Church makes in this matter in twofold. In the first place, the existence of a permanent teaching authority, clear in mind about principles and practical application, with the immense benefit deriving from age-long experience means that, in a world where moral principles are so often at the mercy of passion or self-interest, fixed standards are maintained for a numerically large body of men and women, who may thus hope to present an ideal to those so much in need of one. Secondly, the Church, through her doctrine of grace, holds out hope and encouragement to those who, however clearly they may see their duty, yet come to despair of being able to fulfil it. Indeed it is part of the Church's teaching that the continuous and entire fulfilment of even the natural law is beyond the power of unaided human nature—as the history of the world bears sorry witness. And already at the beginning of the fifth century she condemned the teaching of the Englishman Pelagius that man can find salvation through his own efforts.

The Catholic ideal, then, presents man as in no sense self-sufficient, because, through the Incarnation, he has been caught up into a higher order of existence, nor can he ever satisfactorily be studied apart from that supernatural destiny. Bio-chemistry, biology, psychology, aesthetics, metaphysics may tell us something about him; but always, if we are to see him whole, we must see him at least against the background of the supernatural. Even the pagan philosopher had a glimpse of this. In the last book of the Nicomachaean Ethics occurs this remarkable passage: "Such a life will be beyond the human, nor will it be lived by a man as man, but in virtue of some divine element in him; the activity of this element surpasses that of any other sort of excellence in proportion to its superiority over this composite nature of ours. . . . We should not heed those who enjoin that a man ought to have a man's thoughts, a mortal the thoughts of a mortal, but as far as in us lies he should play the immortal, doing all he can to live in accordance with the highest element in him."*

Whilst therefore the Catholic believes that the moral law is knowable to man by sheer reason and experience, being the law of man's very nature, he believes that the fulfilment or non-fulfilment of it has more than natural implications. The observance of it calls for God's grace; a breach of it is an offence, not against man, but against God, the author of man's nature. Nor is that law a mere catalogue of "Thou shalt not's." "Love is the law's fulfilment" and we must aim at a perfection which is somehow the perfection of God, our Father. In other words, whilst the formulation of the moral law for Catholic and non-Catholic alike may often seem to be made in the same terms, the spirit in which it is obeyed is, ideally at least, a very different matter.

Take for example the question of sexual morality. All men are agreed in regarding adultery and various forms of sexual perversion as wrong; they will seek to avoid such sins from motives which may range from one form or other of self-respect to some vague sense of "playing the game." The Catholic, who is imbued with a conviction of the profound truth that Christ lives on in the members of his Church, will try to take seriously the words of St. Paul: "Shall I take Christ's limbs and make them the limbs of a harlot?" (I Cor. 6 : 15.) So too he will think of marriage as so much more than a legal contract, a solemn pledge of loyalty—though it is indeed that; for him it is a special way of living the Christian life. He will recall how St. Paul sees human marriage as a pale shadow of the bond uniting Christ with his Church, as therefore an immensely sacred thing, to be regarded as a sublime vocation and not as a means to mere physical satisfaction. At the same time, because of the Incarnation in which the human body is ennobled, he will be far from the Manichaean notion which sees physical sex as an evil thing.

For reasons such as these, whilst he may find the demands

* *Aristotle.* Nic. Eth. 1177b.

of God's law hard, he will remember that the loveliest things are hard-won. He will know that, in this intimate mystery in which human life is handed on, he is playing a part which is a kind of symbol of the handing on of the divine life of grace, and will be ready therefore for the highest standards of conduct. Contraception, which frustrates the end and purpose of the natural function, and abortion, which stifles the human life after its initiation, will be for him sins against the temple of the Holy Spirit. Divorce, in addition to being a refusal to honour his word, is also to be seen as a kind of schism in the body of Christ.

So of all the virtues which go to the building of the perfect man—truth-telling and justice, fortitude and temperance, the whole of what Mr. Lewis refers to as 'the *Tao*'*—the Church respects and inculcates every one, because of her high regard for the human nature which they perfect and adorn. It is a part of her holiness that she should do so; though it needs little experience of individual Catholics to teach us how far short of the ideal many of them fall. This is not to excuse them or to belittle the ideal. *Corruptio optimi pessima.* The Catholic is only too conscious of his responsibilities in all this matter.

II. Social Teaching

There is one aspect of the Church's doctrine which in this twentieth century calls for more extended treatment—that of her social doctrine. At the very beginning of this book we said that "the Roman Catholic Church exists to teach men a way of life which is only incidentally related to the social or political condition of this or that epoch" and nothing that we shall go on to say must be allowed to obscure that fundamental truth. Yet because the material upon which she works, mankind, necessarily exists in a certain social environment she cannot but be deeply interested in that environment. Nor can she forget the teaching of her Master that men will be judged according to the way in which they have treated their fellow-men. "I was hungry, and you gave me food, thirsty, and you gave me drink. . . . When you did it to one of the least of my brethren here, you did it to me." (Matt. 25 : 35, etc.)

---

* *The Abolition of Man*, 1943.

We may begin then by suggesting that the Church does not present a ready-made scheme of social reform; she does try to inculcate an attitude of mind which will issue in the right sort of social improvements. When she began her history she was hardly in a position to lay down a scheme of social betterment. A despised and persecuted minority in a ruthless world, the early Christians could hope for no more than to preach a gospel of love and unselfishness which would lighten the burdens of the less fortunate among the brethren. Slavery, for example, was an accepted institution in the ancient world; the whole social and political structure was built up upon its acceptance. What she could and did attempt was to ensure that masters should treat their slaves as fellow-members of Christ. So to-day, whilst Catholics will be found working in different ways for the betterment of social conditions, it would be useless to look for an official Catholic Social programme. Yet in the great social encyclicals of the Popes, beginning with Leo XIII's *Rerum Novarum* (1891), will be found the principles through which lasting improvement has been or might be achieved. The Church maintains, for example, that since man cannot live a human life without being able to call something his own, since he is so made that his life is incomplete unless he has the opportunity and the means of some form of self-expression, the denial to any individual of some form of ownership must be condemned. It follows, therefore, on the one hand, that extreme forms of socialisation, in which no man can be said to have anything at all as his own, are just as wrong as the unbridled individualism, which inevitably results in the exploitation and expoliation of masses of men and women. In the struggle between Capital and Labour, which was one outcome of the Industrial Revolution, the Church saw clearly and taught explicitly that a solution could be found only by some form of co-operation between the two sides—a commonsense conclusion, of course, but one which is based on more than common-sense in the eyes of the man who holds, as Catholics hold, that the bond which unites men in the brotherhood of Christ, is closer and deeper than any economic or social distinctions. To this point Catholic teaching constantly returns.

Thus Leo XIII has no hesitation in affirming "that all the striving of men will be in vain if they leave out the Church. It is the Church that insists on the authority of the Gospel, upon those teachings whereby the conflict can be brought to an end, or at least, rendered far less bitter; the Church uses her efforts not only to enlighten the mind, but to direct, by her precepts, the life and conduct of each and all. . . ."

He then goes on:

"The great mistake in regard to the matter under consideration is to take up with the notion that class is naturally hostile to class, and that the wealthy and working-men are meant by nature to live in mutual conflict. . . . Each needs the other: Capital cannot do without Labour, nor Labour without Capital. Mutual agreement results in a pleasant existence and the beauty that comes of orderliness; while perpetual conflict necessarily produces confusion and savage barbarity. Now, in preventing and doing away with such strife, the efficacy of Christian institutions is remarkable in its variety. First of all, there is no intermediary more powerful than religion in drawing the rich and poor bread-winners together, by reminding each of its obligations to the other and especially of the obligations of justice. Thus religion teaches the artisan to carry out honestly and fairly all equitable agreements fairly entered into. . . . Religion teaches the wealthy owner and the employer that their workpeople are not to be accounted their bondsmen; that in every man they must respect his dignity and worth as a man and as a Christian . . . and that it is shameful and inhuman to treat men like chattels to make money by or to look upon them merely as so much muscle or physical power. . . .

"But the Church, with Jesus Christ as her Master and Guide, aims higher still. She lays down precepts yet more perfect, and tries to bind class to class in friendliness and good feeling. . . . If the Christian precepts prevail, the respective classes will not only be united in the bonds of friendship, but also in those of brotherly love. For they will understand and feel that all men are children of a common Father, who is God; that all have alike the same last end . . .; that the blessings of nature and the gifts of grace belong to the whole human race in common. . . ."

But lest the Encyclical should be thought to consist of a

series of edifying but not truly constructive platitudes, it must be added that the Pope, having pointed out that "to attain the purpose we are treating of, not only the Church but all human agencies must concur," goes on to indicate the ways in which State intervention can help to better the general lot of mankind. A reading of the whole Encyclical* will make it clear that, implicit in the general principles of Catholicism is indeed to be found a practical solution for one of the most urgent problems of our time.

In the end of course the social problem is a moral problem. The unequal distribution of wealth, whilst it is to some extent due to the operation of non-moral causes, is exaggerated by man's selfishness, and its effects cause such bitterness because of the heedlessness and envy of human beings. So an important part of the contribution which the Church makes to the well-being of mankind is through the efforts she makes to educate men in the observance of the moral principles that are the common heritage of mankind. That is to say she is not merely a theoretical teacher of moral truths; she seeks to help men to fulfil them. A word then must be said here about the ascetical side of the Church's teaching. Taking seriously the paradox that if we are to 'find' our lives we must be prepared to 'lose' them, she has from the beginning held up to mankind an ideal of renunciation which to many has seemed pointless or wrong-headed. If there have been excesses within the Church, they have never been officially approved by her; and certainly they have been nothing like the excesses practised in pre-Christian or non-Christian cults. We may say indeed that here is another example of an almost instinctive tendency of human nature, which the Church has taken and trained. Some of the Fathers of the Desert were undoubtedly odd; but from those strange beginnings developed the whole monastic tradition (of which we must speak at some length later) which has been one of the most potent civilising influences in the history of Europe and the world.

The notion, then, behind the ideal of the ascetic is that, if you are to achieve anything worth while, you must *train* for it—the Greek root means just that—and training for anything

---

* A convenient form of publication is that by the Catholic Truth Society, London, under the title *The Condition of the Working Classes*.

generally means giving up a number of things that are incompatible with your present undertaking. Although, as we have already seen, the Church has always resisted the Manichaean view which would make the body out to be somehow wicked, she has always known that you may not just let the body have all it wants. And that will sometimes mean refusing to let it have something which would not in itself be bad for it. Because the Church has a high ideal of marriage, she exalts virginity and celibacy (when freely chosen for the right motive), because she holds that the fulfilment of man's nature which comes with marriage can come even more completely through the positive creative love which puts God first. It is, after all, not through the physical release of sexual union that man's perfection comes, but through the unselfish love so aptly expressed in the married state. Where you get the unselfishness carried so far that it is prepared to forego the immense happiness of marriage and parenthood, then, the Church holds, you get an even higher form of human perfection.

We all know how soft and slack a man can become in his pursuit of mere comfort. And as a sort of natural protest against that, we get the exploits of a Regulus or a Socrates, a Captain Scott or any of the anonymous heroes of Dunkirk or Arnhem. Mankind needs the fillip of such examples. The Christian summons raises the natural achievement to a higher plane. Christ himself registered his protest against the life of mere comfort by his willing acceptance of a life in which poverty and toil and suffering were so richly blended. The Christian ascetic, inspired by the example of his Master, seeks to keep the world lovely and wholesome by his own contribution to the passion of Christ. Where these greater heroes have gone before, it is a challenge to lesser men to emulate them—and Christ— in a lesser way. The Church, then, keeps before the eyes of her children the representation of the Crucified Christ and of the Saints who have imitated him, so that the ideal of selfless devotion to an ideal may not be lost. Whatever may be said of the excesses that may have occurred, there can be little doubt that the world is indeed a happier place because of the lives of self-sacrifice and self-forgetfulness led by the men and women who may or may not figure in the Church's calendar.

CHAPTER FIVE

THE CATHOLIC VIEW OF HISTORY

By the extension of her citizenship to all her subjects, heathen Rome had become the common home and, figuratively, even the local dwelling-place of the civilised races of man. By the theology of the time Christian Rome had been made the mystical type of humanity, the one flock of the faithful scattered over the whole earth, the holy city, whither, as to the Temple on Moriah, all the Israel of God should come up to worship. She was not merely an image of the mighty world, she was the mighty world itself in miniature. The pastor of her local church is also the universal bishop; the seven suffragan bishops who consecrate him are overseers of petty sees in Ostia, Antium and the like, towns lying close round Rome: the cardinal priests and deacons who join these seven in electing him derive their title to be princes of the Church, the supreme spiritual council of the Christian world, from the incumbency of a parochial cure within the precincts of the city. Similarly, her ruler, the Emperor, is ruler of mankind; he is deemed to be elected by the acclamations of her people: he must be duly crowned in one of her basilicas. She is, like Jerusalem of old, the mother of us all.

Bryce, *The Holy Roman Empire*, pp. 312, 313.

It used to be the fashion amongst New Testament scholars to say that the early Christians as a body and even Christ Himself were so convinced of the imminence of the end of the world that they did not envisage the century-long development of the Church into the vast and complex structure it has become. Without going into any great detail about the subtleties of exegesis required for a proper understanding of the passages upon which such a view was based, it will suffice here to say that, for the Catholic, the end of the world *is* always imminent. To anyone who is convinced, as the Catholic is convinced, that the whole time-dimension must shrink to a pin-point when seen against the background of eternity, there is ultimately

E

little difference between a single generation and the lapse of time measured in geological ages. "The shape of this world passes" (I Cor. 7 : 31.) "We have an everlasting city, but not here; our goal is the city that is one day to be." (Heb. 13 : 14.) Inevitably, the Catholic may seem to sit lightly to the occupations and interests that absorb so much of his fellow-men's energies. His sense of proportion is such that he will strive to put first things first.

And yet, precisely because of his profound convictions, no one is more deeply concerned with the events of this passing scene. He knows that, whilst it is true that the next world is more real than this, it is equally true that his destiny and the destiny of his fellow-men in that next world depend upon their conduct in this. More than this, because he believes this world to be the creature of God's love, issuing from his hands at the beginning of time and perpetually held in being by the continuous act of its Creator, he can watch the whole course of history, the interplay of physical cause and human choice, inexorable law and unpredictable decision, as a fascinating revelation of God's providential wisdom and tender regard for his human creatures. Further still, because God himself has entered into history and, in his own person, lives out a human experience and in his Church mysteriously prolongs his life, therefore does all history take on a still greater richness and significance. Only in view of this tension between the Catholic's detachment from the world and his profound concern with it, will it be possible to appreciate at all the role of the Church in the time-process which we call world history.

The Catholic, then, sees the human drama primarily in terms of the endless struggle between God's loving kindness and the folly and pride that would seek to throw off the claims of that love. Like theme and counter-theme, the ideas of Fall and Redemption, of Sin and Grace, express the inner significance of history. And because he is aware that, could he but understand it all, he would come nearer to an understanding of God's purposes, therefore does he study its course with even profounder interest than the mere professional scholar. He may, indeed, be a professional scholar as well as a Catholic and as such his interests will be similar to those of his colleagues but, as a Catholic, he will have a different philosophy of history. For he will see the course of events, not as exemplifying the working out of this or that economic force, ideological conviction or political trend, but as the manifestation of the providence of God.

Yet it would be misleading to suggest that the Catholic is a sort of super-prig or desiccated intelligence, lacking the ordinary human emotions and seeing men like specimens under a microscope. With more reason than the pagan poet can the Catholic claim that nothing that is human does not pertain to him. The waters of baptism do not dilute his humanity and, if Christ could weep over the forthcoming destruction of the city that was dear to all Jews, the Catholic will not be less sensitive to personal griefs. Believing too as he does that the history of the Church is the story of Christ's experience in its mysterious prolongation, the depth of his interest in that story will be proportionate to the depth of his Christian faith.

The high point of that history is clearly the moment of the Incarnation. In his desire to enter more fully into the meaning of that supreme event, he will feel a special interest in the world-picture presented at that time. One of his early memories will be the hearing of the Christmas gospel associating the emperor Augustus and the governor of Syria so closely with the circumstances of the birth of Christ. Nazareth and Bethlehem, Jerusalem and Antioch, Athens, Corinth and Rome, Herod and the Wise Men from the East, Pontius Pilate, Sergius Paulus, Gallio and the rest are names for ever associated in his mind with the event from which all other events are dated. He cannot be interested in the Incarnation without being interested in history. For not merely is the Incarnation part of history; there is a profound sense in which the history of the world is the history of the Incarnation.

What, if anything, does that statement mean? It means that the history of man and the history of God made man are so intimately associated that we can hope to understand one only by understanding the other. Every aspect of human history casts light on the nature of that complex being, man; it is the chief reason for studying history at all. And the more we appreciate the achievements of man in history the greater is likely to be our appreciation of the ideal of all human beings, Jesus Christ. But the obverse is not less true. The more we understand of the character and moral quality of Jesus Christ, the better shall we be able to appreciate the nature and qualities of man.

If then we are to understand man, we shall need to go back to the very beginnings of his story. The Church has always taken seriously the opening chapters of Genesis, not because she considers them a scientifically complete account of the way in which the world began, but because she believes in the essential point of the narrative. It is true that Catholics, like most Christians, have been reluctant to abandon the more obvious interpretation of the narrative of creation; it is true that, again like most intelligent people, the Church has a feeling that the Evolutionists have tended to overstate their case. But she has no objection to the view that man's body evolved from a more primitive type of organism. What she will have no truck with is the suggestion that therefore there is no essential difference between man and beast. Metaphysical considerations come in to reinforce the description given in the Book of Genesis, with its clear indication that man was marked off from the first as a special sort of creature, drawing his body indeed from the 'slime of the earth' but his soul from the life-giving breath of God, existing in a state of superiority over the animals, a companion chosen by God for communion with himself. It is the common view of theologians that man was created in a supernaturalised state, meaning that, however the human organism came into existence, the creature man, body-soul, was from the first, by a special endowment, made by God for the higher life we have already spoken of. That this intention was, by man's choice, frustrated is the meaning of the doctrine of the Fall.

We are not here concerned with theology but history, however closely, on the Catholic view, the two may be connected. The evidence for that earliest history is altogether too sketchy for us to draw a complete picture. All that we need to say is that the account in the Bible squares with the archæological and literary evidence available to entitle us to believe in the existence of a nomadic type of civilisation in the 'fertile crescent' of the Middle East, during the third millenium B.C. Stemming from a common Semitic stock, one single family originated the history of a nation which, however we look at it, fulfilled a most remarkable destiny. Established in a frontier district which was to be marched and fought across by the armies of empire after empire, subject to one victorious people after another, the Jews yet managed to preserve an individuality and a tradition in a way that seems to demand a more than natural explanation. The power of Assyria passed away, leaving small trace upon the face of the earth; the Hittites survived as little more than a dim legend; Babylonia and Egypt impressed the imagination of the Greek and some part of their culture endured. But the contribution of the Jewish people to the content of European civilisation is incomparable. And all because of their preoccupation with God. Such of their literature as we possess is concerned almost exclusively with their relationship to Him. Whether they wrote history or poetry, exhortation or philosophy, their purpose was always ultimately theological. All we know of their building is that, apart from purely practical construction, their whole artistic effort went into the erection of a great temple to God, to be the centre of their whole national consciousness to a degree unparalleled in the history of the world.

Another remarkable feature of the history of this unusual people is the way in which their thought looked forward rather than back. They remembered Eden, as other nations remembered a Golden Age; but they believed that their finest hour was to be in the future. They lived on a promise. It is this promise, of course, which constitutes their characteristic importance. If the Incarnation is the supreme moment of history, all that passed before that event is but a preparation for it. Whatever interest may lie in the story of Egypt or Greece, Carthage or Rome is purely academic except in so far as it is integrated into the stream of human experience culminating in the union of man with God. In his divine nature, the Word Incarnate stands above the stream of history, controlling and guiding; in his human nature he is the heir of the ages. Into what the theologians call his 'experimental' human consciousness, went the memory of his people, the memory of the promise in the Garden, the memory of the promise renewed to Abraham, the memory of Melchisedech and Moses, of Egypt and Sinai, of Jericho, Sion and Babylon. The prayer and praise of the shepherd-boy turned king went to form at the 'experimental' level his earliest religious ideas. He grew up in the expectation of the fulfilment of the promise that had been made to Abraham, knowing himself to be the fulfilment of that promise. In him "history reached its fulfilment" (I Cor. 10 : 11); and not the history of his own people alone.

For it had been foretold that in him the non-Jewish peoples would trust. The pattern was beginning to take shape. The movements of peoples in the dawn of history, the rise and fall of empires, the groping after truth, the pursuit of beauty, the striving for goodness, all were leading up to this achievement. Increasingly had man become aware of his need for help from beyond himself if human life was to be tolerable. The greatest achievements of the human spirit in art and letters, in ways of thought and ways of life, had at their centre a great doubt and a great sadness. Was there no certain answer to be given to the questing human heart, no saving raft on which man might voyage across the menace of life's storms? Was the end of chivalry to be but a bloody death and a gibbering ghost? Was all human wisdom but folly and ignorance, all human beauty but food for the carrion crow? Was the epitaph on human history to be *lacrimae rerum*?

No. Even the poet who brooded most tenderly over the doubtful doom of human kind

could also glimpse the coming of a saviour, the fulfilment of a promise.

attulit et nobis aliquando optantibus aetas
adventum auxiliumque dei—

"even to our hopes has time brought the help of a god in person." All over the known world men were looking for a Saviour; they turned their kings and emperors into saviour-gods, unaware that God their Saviour would come, not in the guise of king or emperor, but as "one of the children of the year." With his birth comes what may be described as the end of the beginning.

What we have been trying to do is to suggest that only in Christ can even pre-Christian history be appreciated at all adequately. Not that we would be taken to imply that none but Catholics have this Christo-centric attitude to history and to life. But what we do suggest most strongly is that this sort of attitude is a part of the Catholicism of the Church, that only by so universalising one's interests and indeed one's learning, as far as may be, can one begin to have that mind which was in Christ—his catholicity of interest, regard, love.

With the coming of Christ on earth it becomes easier in a sense to see history in terms of his personality. Yet, just as, in thinking of pre-Christian times, there is always some danger of thinking too exclusively of the Jewish story as alone significant for the Christian, so do we incline to think too narrowly in terms of the history of the visible Church. If the kingdom is indeed like to leaven, then it is essential to see the interaction between leaven and not-yet-leavened, and to remember the universality of Christ's mission and Christ's message. In St. Augustine's words: "There is today, in our present age, a terrestrial kingdom where also dwells the celestial kingdom. Each kingdom—the terrestrial and the celestial, the kingdom to be rooted up and that to be planted for eternity—has its various citizens. Only in this world the citizens of each kingdom are mingled; the body of the terrestrial kingdom and the body of the celestial kingdom are commingled. . . . There are two cities, for the present mingled together in body, but in heart separated."

It will therefore be characteristic of the true Catholic to enlarge his vision and to see world history still as the struggle of two contending forces, Christ in his Church seeking to propagate ever further in the recalcitrant material about her the life which came into the world with him. "For this Catholic Church," to quote St. Augustine once again, "vigorously spreading far and wide throughout the whole world, uses all who are in error to her own advancement, and to their amendment, when they shall wish to awake from their error. She uses the heathen as material on which to work, heretics as a test of her teaching, schismatics as a proof of her stability, Jews as a comparison to show her beauty. Hence she invites some, thrusts out others, leaves others alone, and of others she takes the lead. To all, however, she gives the opportunity of participating in God's grace, whether it be that they have to be formed, reformed, brought back to the fold or admitted to it. . . . Often, too, divine Providence allows even good men to be driven out of the Christian communion by the all too factious dissensions of carnally minded men. And if they bear this ignominy or injury patiently for the sake of the peace of the Church, and do not give occasion to any new heresies or schisms, they will teach men with what true affection and sincere charity God must be served."

It is clearly impossible to do more than hint at various ways in which we may see this sort of thing happening in the long course of the Church's story. If, for example, we turn to the field of philosophy, we shall see how elements of Platonic, Aristotelian and even Stoic doctrine enabled her to understand a little more clearly the full message of her Master, who may, in his sheerly human experience, never have heard the names of these schools. Paul, it is true, had some acquaintance with them and we find St. John not afraid to adopt the Philonian Logos as a term to apply to the divine nature of his Lord. In the following century, Justin, with a true Catholicity of outlook, explains his own conversion as a sort of philosophical pilgrimage, in the course of which his disinterested search for truth inevitably brought him to Truth itself. Punic background, Roman education, neo-Platonic thought and Manichaean doctrine together helped to fashion the mind of the great Augustine—supreme exemplification of his own statement: "to them that love God all things, not excepting sins, work together to a good end."

A glance, however cursory, at a book such as Gilson's *La Philosophie au Moyen Age* should suffice to restrain those who are tempted to condemn the philosophy of the Catholic Middle Ages as somehow thin and mechanical. The truth is that there was probably never a time in the history of thought when such vigorous and challenging debate combined with a wide-ranging curiosity to produce a school of men, united in their acceptance of certain fundamental truths, yet passionately at variance in their attempts to interpret and explain those truths. If the towering figure of Aquinas has tended to dwarf his contemporaries, let us recall the varied interests and influences that went to fashion him. Born in the reign and kingdom of Frederick II, of a Norman mother and a father who was a nephew to Frederick Barbarossa, he moved in a fantastic world of colourful adventure, however unadventurous he might appear. The Platonic tradition so vigorously supported by Augustine was still the predominant force in philosophy, but Aristotle, interpreted and misinterpreted by Moslem scholars, was returning to Europe. It was Aquinas who made him acceptable to the Church. The philosophy expounded in Catholic universities and seminaries today is largely Aristotelian; but it should be remembered that it is an Aristotelianism interpreted and enriched by men who have been brought up in a tradition which looks back to Augustine and Anselm, Scotus Erigena and Duns Scotus, no less than to the great Dominicans.

There is some justification for the view that, after the fourteenth century, a certain ossification set in in the Scholastic tradition. The fine flower of the Middle Ages was drooping to its death. There was a dearth of great minds to invigorate it. It is true also that the rise of national consciousness tended to obscure the internationalism of the Church. But deeper than all this was a strange and morbid sickness that threatened to twist the orthodox Christian view of life awry. Christianity had begun as a small persecuted minority in a pagan world. It had grown to triumph over that world, but in the course of the struggle it had had to do violent things. To counterbalance the sensual materialism of its environment, it had reacted in the thoroughgoing asceticism of the Desert Fathers, saving man's soul alive by a ruthless denial of bodily comfort. Balance was achieved, but with the coming of the new struggle against the barbarian the emphasis had to be shifted again. A more humane type of ascetic life developed, teaching the rootless nomad from the steppes the virtues of settled and ordered existence. Yet still in the Christian practice of asceticism there was a recurrent danger of excess. Condemned in various Gnostic guises, condemned again in the Manichaean doctrine, that strange hatred of the bodily self broke out again in the eleventh century with the Albigensian plague. With the assistance of the great Dominican thrust, that too was defeated. But something of the poison survived. It showed itself now in a certain fear of life and slackness of nerve. It was as though men were unable to rise to the height of their argument, failing to have the courage of their theoretical convictions.

At any rate, for whatever reason, the spirit of high adventure seems for a time to have departed from the Church, It did not return until the challenge of the Reformation called out the new crusading spirit of the Counter-Reformation and the Society of Jesus. In the need to meet the criticisms of Protestant divines, a re-thinking of the Church's teaching was called for. In that re-thinking, Jesuit and Dominican sharpened their wits against each other as much as against the common enemy. In the sixteenth and seventeenth century a theological and metaphysical revival took place in the Church which, with intermissions, has continued to the present day.

It is true that officially the Church is interested in philosophy only in so far as it is a sort of outwork of theology. The two may be so closely interconnected that certain metaphysical principles, if only negatively and indirectly, will come within the scope of infallible pronouncement. Moreover, in the course of centuries, whilst elaborating her dogmatic and moral position, she has needed to use certain philosophical tools, which have proved most apt to her purpose. She has therefore a preference for the tradition and language of the Schoolmen; and, as we have seen, the history of the development of that tradition has been such that its framework is much more elastic than is sometimes thought. Today therefore the chief exponents of philosophy in the Church will be found faithful to the ancient ways, but with a fertile and flexible interest in developments elsewhere. Since Descartes broke away from the earlier Scholasticism and Kant was roused by Hume from his dogmatic slumbers, a bewildering variety of systems has been presented for the satisfaction of man's desire to solve the problem of reality. It is true that, almost in the nature of the case, exponents of the traditional system are far less likely to achieve notoriety than are the revolutionaries. But the work of a

Maréchal in *Point de depart de la Métaphysique* relating the Kantian Critique to the Scholastic outlook, of a Maritain in presenting and re-stating the Thomist position, of a Gilson in lucid and fruitful analysis of the movement of philosophical thought from the early Middle Ages to Kant show that even those who seek to maintain a tradition are not thereby precluded from positive contribution to philosophical progress. And to show that Catholic philosophers need not belong to a given school the names of Blondel and Gabriel Marcel may be mentioned.

So much then in all too brief outline for the connection between the development of the Church and the development of European thought. It is time to return and take up the story of the Church in the social and political life about her. We may begin by pointing out that the Church did not set out to impose on the world a definite social and political structure. Just as Christ himself was born into a certain situation and lived his life within a framework laid down for him, so has the Church always acted. There are certain principles of conduct upon which she must insist. There are certain values which she must protect. But such effect as the Church has had—and it is immense—has been due to the interaction of men holding these principles and the environment in which they have lived and worked. Take, for example, the situation in Italy at the end of the sixth century. The Roman Empire had ceased to wield effective sway in the peninsula. For more than a century there had been no Emperor at Rome. Justinian's attempt through Belisarius to reconquer the West for Byzantium had failed, and though the exarch at Ravenna maintained a precarious tenure the power of the eastern emperor had to all intents and purposes disappeared from what had been the cradle of the great Empire. Meanwhile the Lombard was strongly entrenched in the North, threatening the independence of the eternal city. In the circumstances the business of maintaining order, of relieving distress, even of supervising the weights and measures used in his diocese fell upon the Bishop of Rome. It was in this way that there came into being that temporal kingdom of the Pope which was to constitute such an important factor in European politics for a thousand years.

Meanwhile in Gaul an event of great importance was having momentous consequences. At the end of the fifth century Clovis, under the influence of his Christian wife, had accepted baptism, thus entitling France to claim the title of eldest daughter of the Church. Monastic establishments had already been set up in Provence and off the southern shores of Gaul and the Christianisation of the country developed rapidly. Gradually as the spiritual authority of the Pope became more widely recognized with the spread of Christendom, and his temporal power in Italy grew, he was called in to act as arbitrator between contending rivals. In the eighth century Frankish arms finally stemmed the onward march of Islam and on Christmas Day in the year 800 occurred the great symbolic event of the coronation of Charlemagne by the Pope. The Roman Empire in the West had returned as the Holy Roman Empire, with its concept of spiritual and temporal power allied for the defence of Christendom and the establishment of the kingdom of God on earth. It was a concept which never fructified, perhaps because it asked too much of human nature; but as a concept it well typifies the theoretical role of the Church in human affairs. As the Vicar of Christ, the Pope had no purely temporal jurisdiction. At the same time, the subjects of the Church were gradually building up a civilised order of society, threatened with invasion from without and disruption from within. The obvious hope for Christendom lay in a strongly organised central civil power, recognizing the paramountcy of the law of God and therefore, in spiritual matters, of his Vicar on earth, capable by its own strength of resisting the outer barbarian and indeed extending the sphere of Christ's sway.

Although the ideal was so frequently rejected in practice, its persistence as an ideal undoubtedly had great influence on the minds and the conduct of men for centuries. By investing the Church of Christ with dignity and honour, it helped men to a greater spirit of reverence and worship of God, whose vice-gerent was enthroned as an earthly prince, supported by the militant power of Christendom; by holding up to these half-tamed savages the ideal of fighting for Christ, it introduced into their lives some beginnings of a notion of chivalrous dedication. Civil war within the Empire, war between Pope and Emperor, quarrels over rights of investiture, marauding Vikings and buccaneering Normans, the greed of commercial empires, dissolute and time-serving Popes, simony and concubinage in the Church at large, all these and a score of other factors which made the early Middle Ages a shocking and sickening time did not entirely obliterate the light of an ideal once seen. Important in the external history of the Church as were the reigns of Gregory VII, Innocent III and Boniface VIII, it is at least arguable that the true achievement of the mediæval system was that, despite all the forces of disintegration and corruption, the unifying power was always present, reconciling the penitent, breaking down the resistance of the sinner, humbling the proud—the power that came from the general recognition that Christ was still active in the world as he had been in Galilee a millennium before. Undying still the echoes of Roland's horn resounded in the ears of Christian men.

Chrétiens ont droit et paiens ont tort.

It is possible to be 'realistic', even cynical, about the Crusades. Much sheer lust for military glory or commercial advantage, much human pride and ambition were undoubtedly present in the hearts of many who took the Cross. It is equally undeniable that many a man left home and family and all that makes life dear because he thought it a monstrous thing that the places hallowed by the presence of the Saviour during his life on earth should be in the hands of infidels. That in an age of savagery and blood, it was possible to get men to respond to such an appeal is a striking testimony to the power of the Church of Christ. And that power never died.

Not merely was the power of the Church kept in being. It grew and spread. That Gregory who, from his sick-bed, organised the feeding of his city and its defence against the Lombards, despatched a group of monks to reconquer our own island, severed for close on two centuries from the centre of the universal Church. Other monks, some from this island, some from the monasteries of Ireland and of Gaul, went out into the heathen lands of Germany during the seventh and eighth centuries to preach the Word of God. Later the Balkan peninsula, Hungary and Poland were won to Christ. Wherever they went, these monks brought with them the arts of peace, the settled way of life, the custom of prayer and work which had formed them. With them too came the establishment of that hierarchical regime linking the furthest outposts of the Church with the centre in Rome. The *res Catholica* which had conquered the *res Romana* had won a victory over the secular enemies of ancient Rome. The organisation and unification which came with Christianity was something that transcended racial and national differences. But national consciousness was already beginning to provide Europe and the Church with fresh problems.

For Catholicism belies itself if it is not capable of taking a universal view. Patriotism is an admirable and a wholesome thing; but it is not enough. It is a part of the tragedy of modern Europe that the unity of mediæval Christendom was split, under the double assault of nationalistic wars and the impatience of reforming zeal. Not that there was no justification for that zeal, nor that the impatience was altogether unpardonable. The fact remains that, owing to the mixture of motives in the human heart and the policy of Catholics who used the religious disturbances of the time to further the nationalistic ambitions of their country, leading up to the horrors of the Thirty Years' War, a great cleavage was introduced into the body of Europe incomparably graver than any caused by the wars of Catholic princes amongst themselves.

There followed, in the Church itself, that siege mentality which must account for some of the perhaps excessive caution and ultra-conservatism which marked the activities of Catholics during the eighteenth and nineteenth centuries. It was a time of defence, of concealment, of waiting. In our own country, for example, when Catholics were excluded from the higher ranks of the professions—even after the time when the mere saying of Mass or the sheltering of a priest were capital offences—it is hardly surprising that they made small contribution to the national achievement. On the Continent the corroding acid of the Enlightenment was eating away the sense of religion in the minds of the intelligentsia and it was difficult

taken from monasteries

for the Church to maintain her old position as the educator of Europe. She had perforce to be content with the humbler role of preserving the faith in the minds and hearts of those untouched by rationalist teaching. The Revolutionary storms that swept over France, Germany and the Mediterranean lands swept away, too, much of the settled order which the Church had helped to create and which she was striving to maintain. She knew that, whatever the defects of the existing order of things, the danger of revolutionary violence was even more appalling. Yet though, since princes and nobles needed her ministrations not less than the rest of mankind, she has often been regarded as identified with the *ancien régime* and the maintenance of aristocratic privileges, the lives of hundreds of obscure priests in the villages and hamlets of the poor show that she remained substantially faithful to her Master's example.

But if she was on the defensive in Europe, elsewhere she was manifesting immense vigour and activity. Even at the time of the Reformation, when the discovery of new lands and the conquests of the European powers opened up new fields, she had launched a new wave of missionaries who, as of old, often went ahead of soldier, trader or explorer. The story of a Francis Xavier in India and the Far East is but one of a thousand that could be told. Spanish noble and ornament of the University of Paris, he looked forward to a distinguished academic career, until the inflammatory zeal of Ignatius Loyola opened up a vista of new worlds to conquer. In ten years, in addition to much administrative work as general superior of the Indian mission, he evangelized the west coast of India, Ceylon, Malacca, the Moluccas, and spent some two and a half years in Japan. Death found him waiting for the opportunity of entering China. On any reckoning his was an immense achievement but, though almost unique in its range, it was fittingly seconded by the thousands of fellow-workers who could not rest until they had brought the good news of Christ to some fresh people. There is no space to recount, save in the most general terms, the heroic story of the succeeding centuries. Missions to the Great Mogul, Europeans living the lives of Brahmins in order to break down prejudice and circumvent the barriers of caste, journeys overland from India to China, with incidental contributions to geographical and philological learning, the details make a bewildering yet fascinating pattern, worthy to rank with the greatest achievements of man.

One story must be told—the account of the Paraguay Reductions. However disinterested and high-minded the missionaries themselves, it has to be confessed that the soldiers, governors and traders whom they accompanied, and who were often the first Christian envoys the natives had encountered, were all too often greedy, cruel and licentious. They exploited the native populations shamelessly and it is hardly surprising that the missionaries complained bitterly of the hindrance thus put in the way of their apostolic work. But in Paraguay they succeeded in carrying through an experiment perhaps unique in the story of Christianity. Instead of allowing the people of the land of Paraguay to come under the ordinary administration of their Spanish conquerors, with the inevitable sequel, they managed to organise them in self-governing communities of free Indians. By a royal decree of 1607, Philip III of Spain ordained that any Christian converts amongst the Indians might not be enslaved and were to be exempt from the payment of taxes for a period of ten years. In the vicissitudes of their story we shall not enter. It must suffice to mention a few facts. In the year 1733, over 125,000 natives were organised into some 30 Reductions. The material needs of the Indians were provided for by a thoroughgoing system of practical Communism, the produce of each community being pooled for the general good. A standing army was raised and trained to resist the attacks both of the hostile tribes around and also of the Portuguese who had by now wrested the control of the neighbouring lands from the Spaniards. A flourishing economic system with a scientific agriculture and even some simple industries turned the whole region into something approaching an ideal state.

We have dwelt at some length on this experiment because it provides an admirable object lesson, showing that where genuine Catholicism is allowed to flourish without interference, it can produce, as by-products of its religious and moral teaching, conditions of material and social well-being which in the circumstances could hardly be bettered. It is necessary to insist on this point, because it is of course a regular accusation against the Church that the lands under its control are invariably backward and unprogressive. The truth is that there has very rarely been a time when the Church has been allowed to put her ideals into practice. In the Middle Ages, whilst the monasteries provided oases of culture and social development in a world that was often in a turmoil of war and pestilence, the monasteries themselves being often the objectives of piratical raids, the fortunes of the populace at large were usually at the mercy of rulers who were far from Christian, save in theory, and whose jealousy of the Church led them all too often to prevent the latter from exercising that mellowing and educative influence of which she was capable. The Reformation, as we have seen, brought such chaos into Europe that the Church is only now recovering. In modern times, if we recall the attacks upon her from all quarters—the Jacobins, the Commune, the secularist Combe laws in France, the Kultur-kampf and Nazism in Germany, the recurrent anti-clericalism in Italy, culminating in the attacks on the Papacy itself by Garibaldi and the House of Savoy, the frequent persecutions in Spain and Portugal, the savageries practised today in Eastern Europe, to say nothing of the general spirit of irreligion and scepticism everywhere prevalent, leading to direct or indirect restrictions on the Church's liberty of action—the surprising thing is not that the Church has not succeeded better but that she has survived and remained as active as she has.

But it is a commonplace with Catholic writers that, since she claims to be the prolongation of Christ's own life, she will not expect to be exempt from the treatment that was inflicted on him. He was misunderstood, persecuted, done to death— and rose again. It is, so Catholics believe, a mark of her origin that she suffers a similar fate. Again and again, from the time of the Roman Emperors, it has seemed that she must perish. Decius and Diocletian decreed her extermination. Diocletian had not been dead twenty years when his successor decreed her official recognition. Arianism seemed destined to seduce the world; but Arianism is little more than an academic term. The barbarians who broke the power of Rome were tamed by

F

her. Islam set out on a career of conquest that for long seemed irresistible; but the future of western civilisation was not to lie with Mahomet. In England in the eighth century as in the fifth, it looked as though the end of Catholicism had come; but the ninth century saw English Catholic culture at its most flourishing. In the tenth century, the corruption of the Papal court combined with the onslaught of the Northern heathen seemed bound to destroy her again; but in that same century the movement of reform was already beginning at Cluny and, though she seemed likely to fall under the power of the western Emperor as had happened at Constantinople, Canossa and Canterbury remain indelible proofs that *qui mange du Pape en meurt*.

It is unnecessary to continue the catalogue. What has been here set down has been said in no spirit of presumption or boasting. It had to be said to illustrate the thesis of this chapter that the Church that owes allegiance to the Bishop of Rome is the manifestation to the world of the continuing activity of Christ in his world. Nor, once again, is this to be taken as implying that the grace of Christ does not operate in remarkable ways outside what the Catholic regards as the convenanted medium. All who sincerely profess the name of Christ will share somehow in his experience. The closer they come to the centre of truth, the greater is likely to be their assimilation to him who came to give testimony to the truth.

CHAPTER SIX

ROMAN CATHOLICISM AND HUMAN PROGRESS

"It is in historic Christianity, far more than in any purely rational creed, that the religion of Progress finds its satisfaction. For here we have not an abstract intellectualised progress but the emergence of new spiritual values in a concrete historical sense. A new *kind* of life has inserted itself into the cosmic process at a particular point in time under definite historical circumstances and has become the principle of a new order or spiritual progress. . . .

"Nor is it only in regard to these ultimate problems that the religion of Progress finds its fulfilment in Christianity. The practical humanitarian aims of that movement, which are responsible for the social reforms of the last two centuries, also need the support of a positive religious tradition. The ideal of a social order based on justice and goodwill between men and nations has not lost its attraction for the European mind, but with the disappearance of the old Liberal optimism it is in danger of being abandoned as a visionary illusion, unless it is reinforced by a renewal of spiritual conviction."

Christopher Dawson, *Progress and Religion* (pp. 245-6).

I⊤ has become almost automatic in us to judge of an institution by its 'practical' results. Does it or does it not 'deliver the goods'? And we have our own ideas as to what those goods must be. Progress means for the majority of men an increase in the supply of material advantages of different kinds. Now it is true enough that civilisation is to be judged partly on the level of its material achievement. We hold that the archæological evidence justifies us in believing that the ancient Cretans were a highly civilised people; we regard the age of the Antonines as superior to the age of, say, the Merovingians. Life in nineteenth century England was obviously preferable to life in nineteenth century Russia. Today, perhaps, the convinced Marxist would declare that Russia is a more 'progressive' country than

England. Yet he would be basing his view on factors other than the purely material, however illogically.

It should be clear from what we have already said that the Catholic Church's attitude to progress and civilisation is likely to be very different from that of the average product of our modern scientific-materialist age, for whom bathrooms and radio sets, motor-cars and canned foods are the criteria of culture. Her chief concern is with the betterment of man as man, and whilst she is fully aware that that betterment cannot be adequately realised without some measure of material advantage, she will not base her estimate of his improvement solely on the level of his material, scientific or even cultural achievement. Yet, even though she builds for eternity and not for time, leaving to others the business of cultivating the temporal fields of human activity, she can claim with justice that, as a by-product of her religious and moral teaching, her contribution to human progress has been of the first importance. She believes strongly in the effects of original sin on human conduct; so that she is not dismayed as the believer in the religion of Progress is dismayed at the sight of the appalling lapses into barbarity which 'civilised man' commits. She knows that human perfection needs the help of divine grace; where that grace is rejected or ignored, there can be no stable condition of things worthy of the name of civilisation. The epitaph of the Enlightenment and of Positivism was written on the walls of Belsen. It is only those who respect the transcendental value of human nature who can be trusted to legislate for man's temporal affairs. The Catholic Church is pre-eminently concerned with the transcendental aspect of man. Therefore does she seek to develop in her children the virtues of justice and charity, of patience and unselfishness, which are the essential prerequisites of peace and the rule of law. 'Progress' is therefore a by-product of Catholicism; but it is an inevitable one.

We consider elsewhere the Church's moral and social doctrine, but it is fitting to indicate here the concrete results of that doctrine in the history of mankind. In pre-Christian times men had occasionally glimpsed an ideal of social justice and within narrow limits had, for a time, realised something of that ideal in practice. In Periclean Athens, for example, the foundations of a human ethic were being laid by a small group of thinkers. But the humanism of that period was blind to the existence of an immense substratum of slave-population. Not man as man, but only the Greek man, possessed worth, even as a citizen of an earthly republic. And the slave-owning system of ancient Greece was extended under the Roman Empire, in which, eventually, the whole population became enslaved to a soulless bureaucracy. The scholar and the poet might continue to sing of the privilege of belonging to that Empire, but it was a dying force even before barbarian invasions and economic crises brought about its final dissolution. Marcus Aurelius might invite men to regard themselves as citizens of the 'Dear city of Zeus'; but there was no enthusiasm in their response. They looked to the State to protect their material possessions from attack and to maintain the conditions for an ordered life: they might perform the due rites which the State religion demanded of them; but they looked elsewhere for abiding inspiration. Humanly speaking, it was this state of mind which explains the success of Christianity.

> "It (the Church) had its own organisation and hierarchy, its system of government and law, and its rules of membership and initiation. It appealed to all those who failed to find satisfaction in the existing order, the poor and the oppressed, the unprivileged classes, above all those who revolted against the spiritual emptiness and corruption of the dominant material culture, and who felt the need of a new spiritual order and a religious view of life. And so it became the focus of the forces of disaffection and opposition to the dominant culture in a far more fundamental sense than any movement of political or economic discontent. It was a protest not against material injustice but against the spiritual ideals of the ancient world and its whole social ethos."
>
> C. Dawson, *The Making of Europe* (p. 27).

When therefore the old order passed away, there was a new social organisation ready to emerge. We have already seen how Gregory I replaced in effect the old Roman Emperor as the authority responsible for the preservation of a settled way of life in the capital. What Gregory did for Rome, bishops and

abbots were to do elsewhere. Side by side with the feudal
hierarchy and to some extent integrated with it, existed the
ecclesiastical hierarchy which, together with the network of
Benedictine monasteries, provided the framework to preserve
and extend the Christian ideal of human life. Leaving aside for
the present the cultural activities of the different ecclesiastical
establishments, it is relevant to our purpose to point out that,
even at the level of the purely material, the debt of Europe to
the monasteries has been incalculable. It was the monks who
cleared forests and turned fenland into orchard, vineyard and
meadow; it was due to their activities that trading centres,
markets, banks and charitable institutions, surviving the
breakdown of political authority in the tenth century, preserved
the necessary minimum of economic structure on which the
future centuries would build.

In the Middle Ages, as national states grew to independence
and importance, the growth of commerce and the establishment of fresh economic institutions became more and more the
business of laymen. But even then, so long as the unity of
Christendom survived, the influence of the Church remained
of the highest importance. By her moral teaching, she controlled
the operations of financiers, whilst the establishment of guilds
of craftsmen was one sign of the way in which the religious
beliefs of the time entered into and affected social and economic
life. Since the Reformation and the exclusion of the Church
from any direct control of industrial and commercial activities,
the rapid development of abuses of every kind, leading to the
modern reaction against the economic liberalism of the nineteenth century, indicates the need for spiritual authority to
control the excesses of the competitive spirit.

Not that there were not abuses in the times of the Church's
greatest ascendancy. There was undoubtedly much misery and
much exploitation in the Middle Ages. But it must always be
borne in mind that the Church's ascendancy was never as
complete as is sometimes suggested, and that for long periods
her liberty of action was hampered by the secular power. The
long struggle between Pope and Emperor and the story of
Thomas á Becket in our own country should help to remind
us of the difficulties with which she had to contend. But what

can be claimed with truth is that where she did have something like a free hand, as in the monastic foundations, the beneficial work she did was immense.

An excellent example of the indirect effect of Catholic Christianity on social and economic life is to be found in the history of slavery. This institution was so embedded in the structure of ancient society that it was impossible for the Church, even after the Edict of Milan, to eradicate it altogether; but there can be no doubt of the direction in which pressure was exerted by her. Apart altogether from the fact that, in her own organisation, slaves were capable of rising to the highest positions, so that there were examples of slaves becoming Popes (Pius I in the second century and Callistus I in the third), her whole teaching was to emphasize the irrelevance of social conditions, to such an extent that it became necessary to warn slaves not to look down on their masters! "Those who are bound to slavery must treat their masters as entitled to all respect . . . Those whose masters belong to the faith must not think the less of them for being their brethren" (I Tim. 1, 1-2), an exhortation which is repeated by St. Ignatius of Antioch (Polyc. iv). Moreover, by recognizing the marriage of slaves as legal and indeed sacramental, the Church removed one of the greatest injustices of the ancient system. The mind of the Church is sufficiently brought out in this passage from a sermon by St. John Chrysostom: "He who has intercourse with the wife of a slave is as guilty as one who seduces the wife of a prince; both are adulterers." In fact, if the Church did not yet explicitly condemn slavery in principle, she went further by acting as though it did not exist. Thus in the Catacombs, there is no distinction between the tombs of slaves and those of freemen. We know that slaves formed a great part of the Christian community in Rome, yet the term slave rarely occurs on funerary inscriptions, and where slaves were martyred their previous condition did not prevent their being singled out for special honour. In the case of two slaves, Protus and Hyacinth, burned alive under Valerian, their remains had been wrapped in a winding-sheet of gold tissue. Of the actual enfrachisement of slaves by Christian masters the record is stupendous. Nor did the Christian slave-owner demand a payment for this act as did his pagan counterpart.

Moreover, under the influence of Christianity, the Roman emperors developed an increasingly liberal policy, and Justinian's Code bears strong signs of the working of the Christian leaven in this matter. Yet even so, the Church was ahead of the legislator: "the laws of Cæsar are one thing, those of Christ another," says St. Jerome. What would have happened but for the barbarian invasions is a matter of speculation, yet it is almost certain that slavery as an institution would have rapidly disappeared in Europe.

But of course the coming of the barbarian Kingdoms set the clock back in this as in so much else. Not only did the number of slaves increase but the legislation referring to them and the accepted treatment of them made their lot immensely harder. The Church continued her good offices on their behalf, partly by actually redeeming slaves through the efforts of clergy and laity alike, partly by setting an example of kindly treatment, partly by her own ecclesiastical legislation. Thus she developed the right of sanctuary for slaves, insisted on the validity of their marriages, forbade the sale of slaves outside the kingdom, thus reducing the slave-traffic, maintained their right to rest on Sundays and feast-days and in every way asserted the principle of the fundamental equality of slave and freeman in the eyes of God.

That Church properties themselves included serfs is an undoubted fact; what is equally undoubted is that the condition of these men was so favourable that, in the troublous times which followed on the breakdown of the Carolingian Empire, we find men voluntarily surrendering their freedom in order to become *homines sanctorum*—'saints' men', since they were regarded as belonging to the Saints in whose name churches were dedicated. To all intents and purposes they enjoyed the privileges of free peasants. The fact that the status of such ecclesiastical serfs was regarded as much higher than that of their brethren on lay estates is borne out by the knowledge we have that where an estate was transferred to the Church, the serfs who cultivated the land were loud in their expressions of joy.

By the Middle Ages then slavery in the full sense had

ceased to exist in most Christian lands, and though serfdom survived, it represented a great advance on the old state of things, in that the serf enjoyed all the basic human rights, except that he might not leave the land he cultivated and did not possess the privilege of disposing of his property freely. But these were small restrictions in comparison with the benefits which he received. Moreover, even serfdom disappeared more quickly from Catholic lands than it did from those regions where the Protestant Reformation took hold.

A revival of slavery occurred with the discovery of new lands in the fifteenth and sixteenth centuries, but the Church's influence was no longer what it had been, and Protestant England was not the least prominent in the new traffic. Meanwhile, the Popes maintained their protests. In 1462, Pius II declared slavery to be a great crime, and repeated condemnations culminated in the demand of Pius VII that the Congress of Vienna should suppress the slave-trade. The work of men like Peter Claver, who dedicated his life to the service of the slaves in the New World, of missionaries in Africa and America, of Cardinal Lavigerie who established his *Société antiesclavagiste* in 1888 with the blessing of Leo XIII, are sufficient to show that Catholics have been in the forefront of the modern humanitarian movement for the elimination of this evil.

We have discussed the history of slavery at some length because it exemplifies the way in which the Church exercises her influence in the sphere of secular activities. She has never claimed to be able to teach, still less to impose, an ideal social or economic system. The principles of social justice she does assert; but their application in the immensely complex field of economic activity is a matter for the collaboration of the legislator, the adviser and the practical man. The pressure of her doctrine is always exerted in the direction of an assertion of the fundamental rights of man as man; the effects of that pressure will naturally only be felt in proportion as men are prepared to pay attention to her teaching. Her chief function is to maintain an ideal and to encourage all men to work towards it. But churchmen as such are not industrialists or economists, any more than they are politicians or soldiers. Their influence therefore in the different fields of secular activity will always be indirect, effected more by way of negative control than by positive enactment except where some fundamental human right is concerned. The Church does not claim a monopoly of human wisdom.

Yet her very concern with ultimate truth and her interest in human development means that, in many ways, she has taken the lead in intellectual and cultural activities. Even the briefest catalogue of her contribution to the various branches of science and the arts will furnish an impressive tribute to her zeal for progress rightly understood. Of the contribution of the Church to the advancement of the physical sciences, it will not be possible to speak without a glance at the accusation that she is opposed to scientific research and has shown herself obscurantist and credulous to the point of imbecility. The accusation is based partly on the fact that from the time of the Christianisation of the Roman Empire until the time of the Renaissance, scientific method was at a standstill, and no major discoveries were recorded, and partly on the erroneous opinion that when men like Galileo were seeking to propound scientific views in advance of the common opinion of the day, they were brutally persecuted and their doctrines suppressed.

In reply to the second point, it is safe to declare roundly that no scientist has ever been persecuted by the Church for his scientific opinions alone. The central doctrine propounded by Galileo was, after all, the heliocentric theory which had been elaborated by a Catholic priest, Copernicus, with the encouragement and assistance of the ecclesiastical authorities of the time. Galileo's offence was not that he propounded an unacceptable scientific theory, but that he ventured into the domain of theology and scriptural exegesis. So long as he confined his activities to scientific research, he found the ecclesiastical authorities, from the Pope downwards, not only favourable but enthusiastic. He found friends in the Sacred College of Cardinals, whilst in a letter to a friend of his he says: "I have had a long discussion with Father Clavius and two other most intelligent Fathers of the same Order. . . . We have compared notes, and have found that our experiences tally in every respect."* Not all Catholics were to prove so enlightened,

*Opere di Galileo (Ediz. Nz. n. 505).

it is true, but to complete the picture it should be stated that one of the earliest attacks on Galileo was from the pen of a Lutheran named Martin Horky, who wrote to his patron Kepler: "I will never concede his four new planets to that Italian from Padua, though I die for it." Legend has turned Galileo into a noble and disinterested scientist, fighting the battle of truth against superstition and ignorance, typified by the Catholic Church. The truth is much more complex than that. There was stupid conservatism and uncritical acceptance of Aristotelian physics in many circles at Rome; but there was also much enlightenment and genuine scientific interest. Had Galileo shown a little more tact and a little less impetuosity, an unfortunate chapter in the history of science would never have been written. But even T. H. Huxley was of the opinion "that the Pope and Cardinals had rather the best of it." And it is surely significant that, whenever this accusation of obscurantism is brought up against the Church, the same two or three doubtful examples are quoted. If the Church were indeed so hostile to science, it would surely be possible to find a larger selection of her victims.

As to the lack of scientific progress during the centuries between Constantine and the fall of Constantinople, the explanation is to be found largely in the conditions of the time. Society was in a state of chaos. For all that, the Church was laying the foundations of future development. The story of the rise of the mediæval universities is enough to refute the suggestion that the Church was opposed to the extension of knowledge. Had it not been for the Church, it would not have been possible for the extensive system of education which came into being during the Dark Ages to have existed at all. Crude and antiquated as were many of the scientific ideas of the time, this was due not to a failure of scientific interest but to a lack of opportunity for experimentation and the general undeveloped state of men's minds. There were, of course, stupid and bigoted Churchmen as there have been stupid and bigoted scientists; neither class is typical. The broad movement of the Church's activity has always been in the direction of enlightenment. What she does oppose is the one-sided intellectualism which sees human perfection in terms of this or that department of learning or aspect of the truth. In an age when the fundamental human values were set at naught, she must be pardoned for not having cultivated the æsthetic, scientific or literary sides of man's activity to the detriment of his more primitive needs.

The Church puts first things first. It was through her cultivation of theology and philosophy that she developed an art and a literature of her own. In his purely ascetic *Confessions*, Augustine may have reproached himself with weeping over the fate of Dido and not over his sins; but he was formed on Virgil and Cicero, and himself made no small contribution to the development of a rhetorical style not unworthy to be set beside the best of his forerunners. Jerome's self-accusation, *Ciceronianus non Christianus*, should not obscure the quality of scholarship in a man who could undertake the task of translating single-handed the Hebrew and Greek scriptures. The encyclopædic knowledge of an Isidore may seem trivial to us; but it manifests a remarkable concern for human knowledge in all its branches. Boethius and Cassiodorus, Denys 'the Areopagite' and Scotus Erigena, Alcuin, Bede and a host of lesser names testify to the truth that, when circumstances permit, scholarship and Catholicism go hand in hand. Such interests were not indeed purely scientific or purely literary; but they included the lesser and were certainly not hostile to them.

The majestic vision of a Dante is an example of the way in which Catholic truth, preserved in a strict and apparently prosaic system of theology and metaphysics, can flower into beauty at the touch of literary genius. Never was there a more Catholic mind; and his genius found itself not despite but precisely through his Catholicism. But if Dante is the supreme glory of mediæval literary culture, there are so many facets to the achievement of his time that there is some justification for the claim which would see in the thirteenth century one of the peaks of civilisation. It is unfortunately true of the Church as of other institutions that prosperity brings in its train the seeds of degeneracy. Man needs the spur of danger or at least of hardship if he is to continue for long to produce his best work. The high achievement of the Middle Ages was followed by a decline in quality and the late fourteenth and early fifteenth centuries are on the whole amongst the most uninspiring epochs in the history of the Church.

The Renaissance came as a vigorous reaction against such lack of vitality; but it would be false to the facts to see in the vigour of Renaissance culture anything inherently anti-Catholic. Indeed had it not been for the intellectual and educational system established by the Church during the preceding centuries, there would have been no home in Europe for the scholars from the East. Whilst it is true that since the fifteenth century a large proportion of poets and thinkers, artists and scientists have been outside the Catholic Church, this fact does not seriously weaken her claim to be the great educator of Europe. The universities were her achievement and even the men who attacked her were, inevitably, at the beginning the products of her own schools and colleges. Where the Reformation prevailed, her task of teaching had to be taken over by others, but despite that her contribution to learning of every kind remains impressive. Amongst modern scientists the list of Catholics is convincing evidence in support of the claim that Catholic faith and scientific endeavour are in no way incompatible. From Copernicus and Boscovich to Mendel and Pasteur, Catholics have played an outstanding part in every field. The facts may be summed up by pointing out that the proportion of Catholic clerics (i.e., excluding laymen) amongst the 8,847 scientists of varying eminence listed in Poggendorf's *Biographisch-Literarisches Handworterbuch* (1863) is nearly one-tenth.

Of the Church's contribution to letters and the arts little need be said. It is universally recognized that, until the Renaissance, there would have been no culture of any kind had it not been for the Church. Whilst we do not claim, of course, that there can be no culture without Catholicism, what is true is, that without Catholicism, European culture would have been a vastly different and probably a much inferior thing. Amongst the influences that went to produce the great works of art from the Ravenna mosaics to the glories of Chartres and beyond, the inspiration and teaching of the Catholic faith coupled with the patronage, technical instruction and material assistance of

ecclesiastical authorities must be reckoned of primary importance. Europe would doubtless have developed a characteristic
art had the Church never existed; but such evidence as we
have from the lands where the Gospel was not successfully
propagated suggests that the development would have been
much slower and much less complete. It is all but impossible
to imagine a Europe that never knew a Giotto or a Fra Angelico,
a Michael Angelo or an El Greco, a Gothic cathedral or a book
of hours, the cultural life of the monasteries or the music of
Palaestrina, the morality play or the Canterbury Tales.

CHAPTER SEVEN

THE CATHOLIC CHURCH AND THE
MODERN SITUATION

AMONGST the many, doubtless apocryphal stories, which are told of Marshal Stalin is one which refers to some discussion in which the Vatican was mentioned. "How many divisions can the Pope put into the field?" was the characteristic question asked by that grim 'realist'. But he is not unique in his attitude. To many spectators of the modern situation, it is always a great difficulty to understand that the influence wielded by the Church in political affairs is not to be appreciated in the ordinary terms. In the first place, although the Pope is an independent sovereign, the Vatican City, which is his Sovereign State, is considerably smaller than Hyde Park in area and numbers its inhabitants in dozens rather than in millions. It has no army, navy or air force; it has no political constitution in the ordinary sense of the term, practically all its inhabitants being citizens of some other country. From 1870 to 1929, in fact, the Pope was to all intents and purposes a political prisoner of the Italian State. The Lateran treaty which ended the intolerable situation created by the expulsion from Rome of the power which had controlled its civil destinies for close on twelve hundred years did no more than allow the Head of the Church an estate which granted him a real independence, indeed, but the merest shadow of political power.

In the next place, by the terms of the Lateran treaty, the Church is excluded from direct participation in political affairs, save at the invitation of the secular power. And in any case, despite the long history of the Papal States, and the intervention in European political activity by many of the Popes of the Middle Ages, political activity as such is no part of the duty of the Church as such. Doubtless the line between the Pope as Bishop of Rome and the Pope as temporal sovereign was often blurred; and it may well be that Garibaldi was one of the many disguised blessings in the Church's history, when he finally ended the power of the Papal States.

For all that, the importance of the Church in the modern world is something which can scarcely be over-estimated. The truth is that all human activity, not excluding the political, concerns directly or indirectly the soul of man. Wherever the soul of man is in question, eternal issues are involved. Wherever eternal issues are involved, the Church has the God-given right and duty to throw her influence into the scale to maintain a due balance. It may sound well to argue that politics is concerned simply with the temporal features of man's environment and that, since the Church's sphere is the sphere of the eternal, she ought to keep out of politics. But any intelligent observer of the contemporary scene realises that, whilst the political debate may seem to concentrate on temporal interests, moral and spiritual implications are almost invariably involved. The emergence of Communism is merely an extreme example of that truth. The Marxist ideology is meaningless if it does not imply that world history is to be understood in terms of a developing mechanical system. Man is of a piece with his material environment, conditioned by it, in the end explained by it. Over against that is the Catholic view that, however important may be the effect on man of his material environment, in virtue of the material coefficient in his composition, there is another, more important, more characteristic element—soul.

Now it is a fact of the highest importance that the Church saw the threat from Communism before any other authoritative body. Already in 1846, before the Communist manifesto, she foresaw danger. In 1864, in an encyclical letter, Pius IX condemned the doctrines of Communism and (absolute) Socialism, because of their preposterous claim that it was the State which gave validity and juridical existence to the family. It is precisely the perversion of the natural order which the Church regards as the ultimate danger in communistic doctrines. The mere sharing out of property is not, in itself, condemned. How could it be, since Christianity began with a form of community of property? But any attempt to impugn the natural superiority of the individual and the family to

political institutions and economic systems incurs her condemnation, because it is an inversion of the true order. By
another of the many paradoxes we have had to note in the course
of this book, it is precisely because the Church treasures the
individual human soul above all temporal advantages, it is
because, in her eyes, there is this ultimate equality between
man and man, that she protects the diversity and inequality as
between man and man in the circumstances of their earthly
careers. These inequalities are the outcome of that diversity of
gifts which is an undeniable feature of human psychology.
Therefore, the Church, who preaches insistently the duty of
the more prosperous to assist the less prosperous, who has
been distinguished from the beginning of her history for
immense works of charity and social service, who threatens the
rich with the threats uttered by her Master, who promises the
kingdom of heaven specifically to the poor in spirit, will yet
refuse to countenance any system which would aim at reducing
all men to a dead level of unimportance.

There is then this great gulf between the Church, which
maintains the high dignity of man, and Communism, which, in
the end, degrades. It is in this sense that we must understand
her condemnation of 'socialism'. Clearly, there is no intention
of condemning the type of socialism which aims at the due
rectification of excessive inequalities in the community, which
maintains that no individual or group of individuals has the
right to hold the community to ransom or to enslave, in effect,
the bodies and minds of human beings. On the contrary, her
whole history from the beginning has been an object-lesson in
practical socialism. All she is concerned to do is to defend man's
right to be human, to be more than a unit in an economic
system, to be more than an item on an actuarial list. But where
socialism is inspired with a conviction of the transcendental
importance of the human individual as such, working for the
harmonious relations between man and man, group and group,
class and class, until the whole community constitutes a unified
and mutually beneficial society, then indeed will she hold out
her hand in blessing to an ally.

Why then is it that the Catholic Church is so often regarded
as 'reactionary', condemned as 'fascist-minded', declared to

G

be on the side of 'privilege'? The answer to that question involves three considerations. In the first place, there are in the Church, as in all organisations, individuals and groups who, for whatever motive—fear, ambition, snobbishness, ignorance, selfishness—fail to live up to the full ideals of their profession. One of the Apostles has become a byword in history for his treachery; but that is no justification for condemning the Apostles as a body. There have been worldly and wealthy Popes and prelates; but the vast majority of Popes and prelates, to say nothing of the priesthood at large, have led devoted and self-sacrificing lives of service of the poor and under-privileged. On any unprejudiced reckoning, it would have to be admitted that the general tendency of the work and lives of members of the Church has been in accordance with the ideals of Christ, though admittedly falling short of what is required of us by those ideals.

But—and this is the second consideration to be borne in mind—prejudice and misrepresentation have entered in to distort the picture. Just as, in the sixteenth century in this country, the monastic system as a whole was condemned for ulterior motives and the scandalous lives of a minority held up as characteristic of all, so has the modern revolutionary held up the few wealthy or selfish Churchmen as typical of all. The Church in Spain or in Mexico was declared to be possessed of immense wealth, because of the few cathedrals and churches which had, in the course of centuries, accumulated treasure from the gifts of the faithful, and because here and there it would be possible to point to individual members of the clergy whose lives were ostentatious or at least too comfortable. It was found convenient to ignore or suppress the facts about the desperate poverty in which so many of the priests were living lives of heroic self-sacrifice. Nor was it allowed to be known that where religious orders, for example, possessed property or investments, these were being used, not for the benefit of the members of the orders, but on works of education or charitable activities of different kinds. Some of this misrepresentation, doubtless, was due to the fact that the forces hostile to the Church were unable to appreciate the value of the sheerly religious work being done by her. They could not see that a great cathedral, raised to the glory of God, and richly adorned, was a national asset as well as an inspiration and a comfort to many whose thoughts were thereby lifted up to the contemplation of an order of beauty, justice and love which they experienced so little in their everyday lives. But much more was due to the malicious and lying propaganda of the forces of anarchy, who saw in the Church a great bulwark of order, civilisation and decency.

Thirdly, then, we must bear in mind that, whilst the Church is committed to the task of working for the betterment of mankind (as Pius XI said: "The Church does not separate a proper regard for temporal welfare from solicitude for the eternal"), she holds that the proper way to achieve this is not by catastrophic violence but by working upon the existing system from within, preserving what is of value and eradicating abuses. She remembers the example of her Master, who rebuked his impetuous disciples who wanted him to destroy a place that did not come up to their standards; she recalls how he likened the kingdom of God to leaven working in secret; she has not forgotten the lesson of the parable of the wheat and cockle: sometimes in eradicating abuses you may do more lasting harm than good. Admitting that the maldistribution of property is a grave evil in the world, she does not agree that the remedy is to abolish property altogether, but to do all possible to eradicate the maldistribution of it. The proper cure for intemperance is not Prohibition. The ideal solution is to train the individual to self-control; until that is achieved some measure of state-control will probably be necessary. Similarly—to quote Pius XI again: "When civil authority adjusts ownership to meet the needs of the public good, it acts not as the enemy but as the friend of private owners."

It is against this general background then that we must try to see the Church's attitude to modern political problems. She does not, as a rule, intervene directly in the ordinary activities of, say, the political parties. When she does so in anything like an official way it is because the issue has risen far above the level of ordinary politics, as in the Italian elections of 1948. There, as all the world knew, what was being decided was not the question whether this or that purely political group was to be charged with the government of the country, but whether a country traditionally Christian was to fall under the domination of a regime that was openly and confessedly opposed to religion in general and the Catholic Church in particular. The triumph of de Gasperi was of profound spiritual significance. In normal circumstances, the Church encourages her children to play their part in politics not by organising specifically Catholic parties—though this has happened on occasion—but by conducting their civic and public activities in a spirit consonant with the principles of the Gospel.

Thus, to take our own country as an example, apart from occasions where specifically Catholic interests are involved, as in the case of successive Education Bills, the Catholic hierarchy has not pronounced in favour of either of the major political parties nor has it, except in the most general terms, ever directed or suggested the way in which Catholics should exercise their right to vote. Catholics are found on both sides of the House. The fact that more M.P.'s are to be found on the labour benches is to be ascribed not to any political bias in the Catholic body so much as to the overwhelming predominance of the working-class in the Catholic Church. It is, too, traditional in this country that the clergy do not associate themselves with any political activity, whatever may be their personal views, still less do they stand for Parliament. On the Continent this rule is not so scrupulously observed, though the participation of priests in direct political activity is discouraged.

It is in the sphere of international relations that, from her very nature, the Church is able to exercise the greatest influence. Over against international Communism, with its disintegrating and subversive tactics, she opposes a doctrine of true universal brotherhood, which, whilst taking full account of local and national loyalties, is yet insistent that, since these themselves are rooted in the nature of man, they should not in any way conflict with the higher loyalties involved in the acceptance of the general fatherhood of God. It is by now notorious that where a country turns Communist it ceases to live an independent and individual life. It must be so, since national political activity and international Communism are exercised in the same medium—the economic and social conditions of human existence. But, precisely because the Church's primary interest is other-worldly, so that she can maintain a certain detachment from the material conditions of this present life, because she finds the basis for common action in the universal qualities of human beings as such, far from needing to set class against class, to exploit grievances, to dissolve away the natural loyalties, she is all the time preaching and working for the universal good of all men. Such universal good is not to be achieved by the disappearance of the lesser advantages to be derived from local organisations and local differentiation. On the contrary, it is inherent in man's nature that he love the immediate and personal object of attachment. It is not without significance that, where the Communists sought at first to undermine the natural affection uniting members of the family, and by a sexual doctrine which would ruin the whole fabric of marriage, to corrupt human nature at its roots, the Church has, from the beginning, seen in the defence of the family, the surest defence of all the natural human institutions.

In passing, then, it may be well here to glance at a common objection which is brought against the Catholic Church, particularly in this country. It is often said that there is something 'un-English' about her; and references are made to the 'Italian mission'. At the time of the restoration of the Roman Catholic hierarchy in England in 1850 there was much talk of Papal 'aggression' and though such language has been proved by the event to have been exaggerated to the point of hysteria, there are still to be found those who assert or imply that loyalty to the Catholic Church is incompatible with full patriotic loyalty to this country. In the first place this is belied by the facts. During the war with Hitler, there was no Englishman more forthright in his patriotism and more vigorously active in support of the country's morale than the late Cardinal Hinsley, whilst it is a matter of public record that the percentage of Victoria Crosses won by Catholics was considerably higher than the proportion of Catholics in the total population. In all walks of life are to be found Catholics wholeheartedly devoted to the well-being of the country. Their record, in law and medicine, in politics and letters, in education, industry, sport and every typical English activity, is incontestably good.

Nor is this unexpected. Catholicism teaches that all lawful authority is of divine origin, and therefore temporal rulers are to be obeyed with scrupulous exactness. It teaches that man's social institutions exist for the development of man's nature, and the Catholic's co-operation is therefore a part of his plain duty. The same considerations apply of course to Catholics of other countries. Since the Englishman prides himself on his patriotism, he ought not to misunderstand manifestations of patriotic fervour by Catholics of other countries. He is pleased when the religious leaders of his own country bless the undertakings of his own nation. But when Catholic bishops in other countries manifest a similar patriotic spirit he is apt to be suspicious and resentful where those countries are pursuing policies that do not commend themselves to him.

Let us now return to the consideration of the Church's international influence. The time is rapidly approaching when the international tension will be manifested for what it is—a cleavage between those who aim at the enslavement of the human spirit to a soulless ideology and those who believe that man can be liberated only by the cultivation of true spiritual values. In the defence of those values the Church believes herself to be endowed with special powers and a special commission from her Master. Therefore does she invite men of goodwill everywhere to associate themselves with her in this supreme task. But she would be stultifying herself and denying her origins if she did not insist on her position as the sole fully authentic Christian institution. And when members of other bodies resent her action in refusing to submit to their leadership, let them reflect that they themselves have shown little readiness to respond to her invitation to form a united Christian front. More than once has the Pope called on all men of goodwill to unite in face of the common enemy. Such a unity, if it is to be established, can only come about through the acceptance of certain clearly formulated principles of belief and action. In the nature of the case, it is for her to state the principles according to which she must act. If others refuse to accept them, she must regretfully but firmly reply that the ground of common action does not exist. She respects the sincerity of others; she can only ask them to respect hers.

In the meantime, in virtue of his accepted position as the spiritual head of some three hundred million Catholics scattered throughout the world, the Pope is in a position to exercise an immense if indirect influence on the course of human history. It is for this reason that the Church is regarded by the materialist and the sceptic as the great enemy. She is indeed the enemy of the enemies of mankind. It is a familiar role. Whatever be the outcome of the present struggle she can face it with confidence, knowing that the gates of hell shall never prevail.

CHAPTER EIGHT

CATHOLIC LIFE AND PRACTICE

To see Catholicism in the round it is necessary to get away for a time from the general account of movements and tendencies, history and theology and the rest and try and see what life is like for the average Catholic. What is there that is peculiar to him that makes him different from his fellow-men? Once again, a serious difficulty arises from the fact that in detail much of what we shall describe as characteristic of the Roman Catholic way of life will be claimed by others as possessed by them. Once again, the answer must be that it is the totality which must be looked at, whilst it is not unfair to suggest that, quite often, where there is question of some specifically Catholic practice, shared by those outside Roman Catholicism, these are, to that extent, Roman Catholic *manqués;* that in so far as they believe in such practices, they are in line with the great Catholic tradition which has developed from the earliest centuries down to modern times.

Take for example the most characteristic of all Catholic activities—the Mass. It is true that not a few who do not regard themselves as owing allegiance to the Bishop of Rome, claim to say or hear Mass with as much devotion and faith as the most pious of Roman Catholics. Yet for all that it is a specifically 'Roman' Catholic belief, since it developed under the guidance of the Holy Spirit during the centuries when Catholicism and 'Roman' Catholicism were one and the same. From the Last Supper to the latest decree of the Sacred Congregation of Rites there has been an uninterrupted process, going on within the Church centred in Rome, which has given to the world the Mass as it is known today. It is not less specifically Catholic because it is adopted by those who reject the authority which was responsible for its growth any less than an Old Etonian tie remains what it is, however widespread its use may become amongst those who have never set eyes on Agar's Plough.

With that said, let us turn to the business of sketching the life of a Roman Catholic, admitting that it may not always be easy for others to see why we claim this or that item as peculiar to the Church. Admittedly too such an attitude may seem arrogant to the point of uncharitableness. We can only plead that it is in no spirit of arrogance that we seek to state the facts as we believe them to be.

Perhaps the main characteristic of his religion as it strikes the individual Catholic is that it is an activity exercised in common with others. Whatever truth there may be in the dictum that "religion is what a man does with his solitariness," the Catholic on the whole finds himself most truly religious in his corporate worship. He takes very seriously his profession of faith in 'the communion of saints', thinking of himself as a member of that vast household of God, which reaches into heaven, where the Church triumphant enjoys the beatific vision, and stretches out to the furthermost limits of the earth, where he knows that the central act of worship, the Mass, is being offered "from the rising of the sun even until its setting." In that sacrifice, annihilating space and time, he believes that he draws near to, is indeed personally associated with, the death of Christ himself, perpetually offered for the salvation of the world. The very language in which the liturgy is performed, the stylised actions, the traditional vestments remind him of the earliest ages of the Church. He is one with the outlawed Christians of the Roman Empire, offering this same sacrifice in the catacombs or in the houses of noble ladies, one too with the Pope himself, offering it in far-off Rome, in all the splendour of the full Papal liturgy; he is one with the missioner in remote Alaska, with the prisoner in Dachau, the exile in Siberia. He remembers John Sobieski, hearing Mass before he drove the Turk back from the walls of Vienna, he thinks of the men who have died a martyr's death in order that the Mass might not cease.

It is unnecessary to add that these thoughts are not usually present to the consciousness of the individual Catholic whilst he is hearing Mass. But it is true that the liturgy has, as it were, soaked in all these associations in the course of the centuries and that the simplest Catholic child is given some idea of the historic wealth they contain. He is taught that the vestments which the priest wears derive from the dress of the Roman people at the time when the liturgy was becoming fixed. He may have very little Latin himself, but he takes pride in knowing that, in listening to the familiar words spoken by the priest at the altar, he is listening to the language which was spoken in Rome and the West when Christ was on earth, the language which figured in the inscription over his Cross, the language which was for so long the common language of Europe. In the liturgy too are embedded fragments of Greek and Hebrew, the other elements of the inscription written by Pilate. It is all strange and unlike ordinary life, you might think; but it has become so much a part of ordinary life for him, that its familiar strangeness is undoubtedly of the first importance in developing in him that consciousness of living in two interpenetrating worlds which is of the essence of the Catholic mind.

Nor, although he naturally values the solemnity and dignity attaching to liturgical services as they are performed in the grandeur of some historic Cathedral, is he particularly distressed that, so often, his church will be small and undistinguished, sometimes even mean and ugly. He would like things better; but he recalls that his Church began its life in a stable and has so often lived a hunted and underground existence that this too all fits in. In spite of the common opinion that such success as Catholicism has had is to be attributed to its 'sensuous appeal'—incense and candles, rich vestments and operatic music—it is on the whole truer that the very poverty of the Church demands of its members an austere standard in the matter of accessories to worship. Nor is this unhelpful. Since the Catholic believes that he is present at the tremendous mystery in which the Godhead is veiled under the appearance of a wafer of bread, he will not concern himself over much with appearances.

So important does the Church believe the Mass to be, that it is her law that all those members of her flock who have attained the age of reason, and are not prevented by sickness, urgent and necessary business or some other compelling cause, are bound to attend Mass every Sunday and on seven or eight major feast-days during the year, under pain of mortal sin.

This may seem a harsh enactment; but by the maintenance of a high standard of regular observance it is possible for man to rise to the height of his nature. The Church holds that the very fact of God's existence makes stern demands upon human nature. Only in so far as man lives his life in accordance with truth can he be fully human. The supreme truth is this truth about God. Therefore must man make some acknowledgment of his existence.

Theoretically no doubt it would be possible for man to fulfil all justice in this regard by his own private devotions. But experience shows that such private devotions do not, for most men, long survive without some sort of sanction. Moreover, man is more than a solitary individual; he has a nature which can only be satisfied in association with others. Friendship, marriage, the family, political organisation, the club, all these are so much a part of human life that, if they were taken away, life would cease to be truly human. So in the matter of religion. Take away the social aspect of religion, the Church holds, and you dehumanise man in the most important aspect of his life. There are other reasons which can be appreciated only when we have spent some time on a study of the theology of the Mass. For the present it will suffice to say that such is the Church's law; every Catholic regards it as the test of his fidelity.

When actually at Mass he may not feel any very great personal devotion; he may be sleepy and distracted, conscious it may be of a sinfulness which prevents him from making that wholehearted surrender of himself which this sacrifice of its nature demands. He may even feel a vague resentment at being compelled by the Church's law to assist Sunday after Sunday at this cold, impersonal, hieratic ritual. But in his heart of hearts he knows that it matters more than anything else on earth, that the effort required of him is but a small price to pay for the enormous privilege it implies. About him he will see men and women of every kind and degree, the intellectual, the fashionable, the poor; members of the professions, members of every political party, members of every kind of social organisation; children barely able to walk, old people on the very edge of eternity—a perfect cross-section of mankind, the only complete democracy. For, in face of what is being done here, no human distinctions matter at all.

But not merely is the Catholic conscious of this great fellowship in common act of worship. There is too a Catholic mind, a way of looking at things, which he shares with all who belong to the Church. Obviously, the highly intelligent and the professional theologian will have a more articulate appreciation of the technical sense of certain dogmatic definitions. But where you are dealing with mystery, intellectual endowments do not make all that difference. All Catholics capable of intelligent thought subscribe to the same doctrines, taught in the same sort of way, stated in a common language. They know what the priest means when he pronounces the Creed; they know that all Catholics from the Pope down to the humblest school-child accept that Creed in its fulness, without reservation or gloss. Most of them would not pretend to know—so as to be able to put into words—the full content of the Catholic faith. What they do know is that, whatever that content may be, it is accepted without demur by the hundreds of millions constituting the Church at the present day, even as it has been accepted from the beginning.

A word then about the Catholic's attitude to his faith. In the first place, he understands that it is not primarily a matter of intellectual appreciation. Faith is a decision of the will, based on an intellectual process, but going far beyond what the intellect can understand. He sees enough to satisfy him that, in making this surrender of his will, he is not stultifying himself. That he should believe seems to him entirely reasonable, even though what he is called upon to believe is so far beyond the reach of reasoned argument. In fact it seems to him entirely reasonable that there should exist truths beyond the scope of his mind. For what he believes is nothing less than the truth about God, about creation, about himself. A decent modesty might prompt him to reflect that he could hardly hope to understand all that. He finds himself baffled in his attempts to understand the everyday world about him; it seems to him therefore most probable that, when he comes to reflect on the world beyond this, he should encounter mystery.

Using his reason as far as it will go, studying such evidence as is available to him, he comes to what is for him the inevitable conclusion that religion has to be taken seriously. God exists. That fact alone matters. Or if other facts matter, they matter only relatively to it. Convinced that God exists and that his own existence is secondary to and dependent on God, he has no difficulty in supposing that the truth about himself, about life, about the world, is to be sought somehow from God. He finds himself normally living in a family or a group which accepts, as from God, a whole range of statements which form a satisfying and coherent system. If he rejects them, he cannot find any more coherent or satisfactory explanation of himself and the world. There are details in the system which puzzle him; there are demands made upon him which he does not entirely relish. There will be times when he wishes desperately that the whole thing were not true. He has to confess, a little wryly, that when he is accused of wishful thinking in thus accepting God and the Church, he cannot help feeling that wishful thinking would be likely to produce a less exacting form of discipline.

For of course faith does make demands. It is not merely that membership of the Church involves certain obligation over and above the ordinary obligations of the moral law. After all, membership of any organisation is likely to do that. It is rather that faith itself, wholeheartedly accepted and seriously lived, requires a constant vigilance and a constant effort at growth. It is just not true that the Catholic faith is a series of antiquated, rigid and rather meaningless propositions, to be accepted in a spirit of blind and uncritical acquiescence. So alive and actual is it that only by a corresponding vital effort can the Catholic hope to live up to it. Hence it is possible for him to fail to increase in stature in accordance with its requirements, to grow away from instead of up into the faith, and to lose touch with it to such an extent that it does become a burden rather than an inspiration. Eventually, as sometimes happens, the faith is lost. But the fault lies not in any unreasonable demands it makes but in the moral failure of the individual.

Of the content of the faith we have spoken in some detail in an earlier chapter. Here we are concerned to note the central place which faith itself holds in the make-up of the Catholic.

It is a skeleton which gives shape and strength to his life; but not a skeleton in a cupboard. If at times the Catholic is made to look a little out of date because he has not read the latest book on biblical criticism, preferring it may be to read the Bible itself, he will not worry about that unless he is an intellectual snob. He rests in the secure belief that no sort of truth can conflict with the word of Truth itself which is the content of his faith.

For the Catholic believes what he believes, not just because he is told to believe by the Church authorities, any more than the good citizen keeps the law just because there is a policeman at hand to enforce its observance. Behind the policeman is the authority of the State, acting for the common good; behind the Church authorities is God. The ultimate motive of faith is the veracity of God. One common misrepresentation of the Catholic position is the statement that Catholics are not allowed or encouraged to read the Bible. This certainly is untrue. Not only are Catholics encouraged and expected to read and study the Bible privately but extracts from it form considerable portions of the liturgy at which he assists. What is true is that the Church values so highly the revelation of God contained in the Bible that she will not allow irresponsible criticism and interpretation of its contents. Just as the law and constitution of the civil state is safeguarded by the work of experts upon it, and nothing but confusion and anarchy could supervene if 'private judgment' were given its head in that sphere, so does the Church hold that the immensely subtle points of doctrine implied in the Bible literature need to be studied and interpreted by those who are most competent in the matter. There is sound Catholic sense in the words of Oliver Goldsmith: "As I take my shoes from the shoemaker, and my coat from the tailor, so I take my religion from the priest." The Catholic knows that where points of faith are concerned no man is, of himself, adequately equipped to pronounce a verdict, and he is content to allow the patient work of the scholar, controlled and directed by the wisdom and experience of the age-old Church, to elucidate for him the sense of the words of Moses and the Prophets, of Christ and his apostles.

In virtue of his faith, then, he moves about in worlds not realised, and for that reason may at times seem to be out of touch with what is called reality. It must be so, when human beings attempt to relate the temporal to the eternal, the visible to the invisible, the natural to the supernatural. The Catholic is convinced that the natural can be the vehicle for the supernatural; but he also knows that it is a vehicle and not a substitute. We have already discussed the doctrine of the Sacraments, in which this truth is supremely manifested, but it may be well here to say something about Catholic devotion to the Saints, with its collateral question of the use of statues, and other such aids. In the Catechism which every Catholic child learns in his early years, he is taught: "We do not pray to relics or images, for they can neither see nor hear nor help us." Despite much talk of Catholic image-worship and idolatry, therefore, it should be clear that there is nothing freakish about these paraphernalia of Catholic devotion. On the contrary, the use of visible representation of Saints, the veneration of their relics, the massive appeal to the imagination which the Church makes are all entirely consonant with the ordinary characteristics of human psychology. There is no essential difference between the statue of St. Joseph before which the Catholic prays and the statue of some statesman decorated by his followers with flowers on appropriate days. The statesman is being honoured, and his admirers draw help and inspiration from the memory of him recalled by his statue. The Catholic is likewise doing honour to the saint, and, believing as he does that the saint is interested in the well-being of every member of the Church—of which he too is a member—he hopes that his prayers will be heard.

Similarly with the relics which have evoked some derision from the unbeliever. It is surely extraordinarily illogical to establish museums for the preservation of, say, the relics of Nelson—the sword, the cocked hat, the bloodstained coat— and then sneer at others for treasuring the objects intimately associated with men and women whom they believe to have been amongst the greatest spirits of human history. Even 'flesh and bone' relics have their counterpart in the lock of hair cherished by the lover. Affection can often seem a little extravagant to those who do not feel it themselves; but good taste prompts us, as a rule, to respect the feelings of others and any expression of them which does not go beyond the bounds of what is decent.

What is so often overlooked by those whose acquaintance with the Church is superficial, is that just as she was for centuries the educator of Europe in philosophy and letters, so was she the great artistic and civilising force. By one of the many paradoxes that are such a feature of her history, although she set out to preach a Gospel of a heavenly Kingdom, implying the all-but non-existence of temporal values, although for a time she set her face against the art and culture of the pagan world, yet in practice she did come to be the matrix within which were fused Greek and Roman elements to produce a wholly new development. Catacomb painting represents the earliest attempt at a specifically Christian subject-matter, though the artists worked in the contemporary convention. Yet that convention belonged to an already decaying culture and it was perhaps necessary that that culture should die in order that something vital should emerge. During the centuries of the barbarian invasions and the establishment of Gothic and Vandal kingdoms to replace the Roman Provinces in the West, it is hardly surprising that relatively little artistic achievement can be recorded. Yet the seed which was saved when the ancient growth withered was germinating underground. Whatever had life in the old culture was protected by the Church which knew that all beauty is a manifestation of un-created Beauty, and when the time came it flowered anew.

In the East, meanwhile, where the ancient forms were being adapted to serve the new truths, the great Iconoclastic struggle might have struck a fatal blow at Christian art, had not the influence of the western Church been thrown into the scale in defence of man's right to paint pictures and fashion statues that might portray the objects of his worship and veneration. That achievement in itself is of immense value, at a time when the poverty of the West precluded the production of great works of art. Not that positive achievement was not realised. It was the age when the beauty of liturgical expression was being developed, in the decoration of vestment and altar, in the

elaboration of the basilica style and the creation of a musical
style to match the austere restraint of the Roman ritual.

However, we must leave for the present a fuller discussion
of the part the Church has played in the history of art. What we
have said here will suffice to remind those who need reminding
that the Church, in her attempt to realise the perfection of
man, is aware of the almost infinite complexity of human
nature and the manifoldness of his needs. She is directly and
fundamentally concerned with his eternal welfare. But she
knows him to be a creature of time, immersed in a material
world, composed of body no less than of soul. She is moreover
concerned with men and women of every degree of intelligence
and taste, so that the sophisticated will sometimes condemn the
crudities of Catholic taste, whilst the half-educated will think
of her as remote from ordinary life. They will find in the average
Catholic church much that will puzzle them, and on a first
acquaintance with Catholic teaching they will be liable to
condemn much of it as nonsense. But the Catholic himself is
entirely at home in his church and, whilst he knows that his
faith is full of mysteries, he knows too that they are beyond
his comprehension, not because they are nonsense but because
his mind is incapable of grasping infinite truth. It is precisely
because much of the intellectual content of his faith is beyond
him that he feels at home with what we may call the furniture
of the faith—statues and stained-glass windows, holy pictures
and his rosary. He knows well enough that the reality is not
like that; it would not be very much more like it, if the most
perfect artistic standards were always maintained in ecclesiastical art. Perhaps his taste is not very good. He certainly does
not believe in art for art's sake. But if, in his simplicity, he
finds inspiration or comfort in some inartistic portrayal of
what is in any case incapable of portrayal, the critic may be
silenced by the reminder that a certain childlikeness of mind
is demanded of those who would enter the kingdom of heaven

As we have mentioned the rosary, one of the most familiar
objects of piety in the Catholic Church, some words of explanation will not be out of place. Its structure—five decades of
beads, strung on connecting links of wire—is associated with
three groups of five incidents or 'mysteries' in the life of Christ.

H

Whilst reciting the appropriate prayers, the person praying will be thinking over or picturing to himself the appropriate mystery. Thus the first item of the first group of mysteries, entitled the 'Annunciation', invites us to think over the beginning of the Christian story, when the Virgin Mary was told by the angelic messenger of God's purpose in her regard. The decade begins with a recital of the Lord's Prayer, which is followed by the Hail Mary, repeated ten times whilst the mystery is pondered. In all these five 'joyful' mysteries, concerned as they are with the conception and birth of Christ, it is natural that the Church's prayer to God's Mother should provide the verbal background against which is set the picture being contemplated. To some it may seem out of place that, when the incidents of Christ's Passion, culminating in the Crucifixion, are the subject of meditation, the prayer-formula should still be the same. For the Catholic, who never finds Mary out of place, since she above all creatures was most intimately associated with Christ in all his works and sufferings, there is no sense of inappropriateness, still less of distraction. He is thinking of him along with her; in her company he knows that he will better realise who and what he was. Lastly come the 'glorious' mysteries, recalling the triumph of Christ in his Resurrection, shared with his creatures and supremely with his Mother. In its combination of simple pictorial imagination, combined with profound theological truth and held together by the familiar prayer-formulas, the rosary carries an appeal to every type of mind. Traditionally associated with the name of St. Dominic, though historical criticism suggests that it was one of his sons who popularised it in the fifteenth century, it has undoubtedly been a remarkable force in developing habits of prayer amongst Catholics of every degree in every country. "The objection so often made against 'vain repetitions' is felt by none but those who have failed to realise how entirely the spirit of the exercise lies in the meditation on the fundamental mysteries of our faith. To the initiated the words of the angelical salutation form only a sort of half-conscious accompaniment, a bourdon which we may liken to the 'Holy, Holy, Holy' of the heavenly choirs and surely not in itself meaningless."

Having thus introduced one specific form of prayer, we may suitably continue to discuss the general subject of prayer in the Catholic Church. Prayer is a feature of religion of any vitality. What is there to be said specifically about Catholic prayer? It is a part of the perennial paradox of the Church that, whilst her official prayer is liturgical and public, she of all the Christian denominations has most effectively developed in her members a personal interest in prayer and produced mystics of outstanding eminence. Whilst admitting the reality of mystical experience amongst those who belong to the eastern religions and whilst remembering the genuine strain of mystical communion which appears to have been realised by Plotinus and some of the great neo-Platonists, we may be pardoned for pointing out that any history of mysticism inevitably draws largely on the doctrines and experiences of the great Catholics such as Juliana of Norwich and the English school, Ruysbroek and the German, and supremely, of course, St. Teresa and St. John of the Cross, the great mystical doctor. In this department as in so many others, it is the Church that has fostered and protected a tradition which, however consonant with the needs of human nature, does not, as a matter of experience, flourish save where there is a regular discipline and an organised control. It might seem presumptuous, to some who reject the name of Roman Catholic and yet claim with justice to be leading lives of prayer; yet it is not unfair to say roundly that nowhere save in the Church is there this permanent interest in and general encouragement of every type of personal and individual prayer.

We say every type of prayer because there is an ascending scale of prayerful activity, from the simplest utterance of a consecrated formula to the highest reaches of mystical union with God. We have seen something of a simpler type in discussing the rosary. The liturgy to which we have referred represents another state of prayer. Of mysticism we have perhaps said as much as is called for in a book such as this. But for even the barest sketch of Catholic prayer it will be necessary to add some lines on the subject of meditation. Because the Catholic holds that his religion is not merely a matter of external observance but demands an assent of his will to certain truths, because he realises his oneness with the great movement of God's grace in history, operative especially in certain outstanding figures, above all because he holds with intense conviction the historical actuality of Christ's earthly experience with its infinite importance to his own destiny, therefore is he required to deepen his appreciation of all these events and truths by deliberate reflection upon them. Such practices are of course no novelty in the Church, but it is to Ignatius Loyola in the sixteenth century that she owes what we may call the popularisation of them.

The instrument of this popularisation is known as the Spiritual Exercises. The method of the Spiritual Exercises is the method of the 'retreat'. Clearly, the idea of withdrawal from ordinary activities for a longer or shorter period of time in order to devote oneself to the thought of God and the truths of revelation is not to be attributed to him; it is not even a specifically Catholic practice. But the organisation of it on any considerable scale is certainly due to him and his followers. The book of the Spiritual Exercises is a short volume, containing outlines of meditation on the Christian truths, beginning with God and man's creation and ending with the idea which is behind all religious activity—the thought of the love of God, using the term in both its objective and its subjective senses. In addition to these meditations, which are the central core of the work, there are considerations on different aspects of Catholic practice, the psychology of conversion, methods of prayer and the like.

In a retreat, whether performed by a single individual or by a small group, the conductor of the retreat expounds to his audience several times a day a selected number of these meditations, according to the length of time available for the whole retreat. The purpose of this—a purpose which is achieved with quite extraordinary regularity—is to deepen the individual Catholic's hold on the truths of his faith and thereby intensify his own spiritual life. The method has been taken over by members of other than Roman Catholic circles, but in essence and in derivation it is a purely Catholic thing.

It should be made clear how little of all this imposed. Despite the common view of the 'iron discipline of Rome', the average Catholic is conscious rather of an immense liberty in his approach to God. Because of the very solidity of the foundations on which his religion is built, because of the hard core of belief and the minimum of essential practice, he enjoys a sense of security which allows him to expand and grow, set free from the restraint which besets those who are in a state of uncertainty and doubt. He appreciates the profound justice of Christ's words: "The truth will set you free." He enjoys supremely that "glorious freedom of God's sons" which St. Paul speaks of. In spite of much modern psychological theory, the happiest children are those who know a reasonable amount of strictness in their education. The best fighters are those belonging to the regiments with a tradition of rigid discipline. And indeed those best acquainted with the members of the Church find amongst her members such rich and diverse personalities that they are merely amused at the pity or the rage of those who would set them free of their 'chains'.

It is said for example that the Catholic Church is 'priest-ridden', that the layman has no say in his religious activities, may not think for himself. We have already (p. 31) discussed this question of liberty of thought in the Church, pointing out that, whilst it is true that there are certain fundamental truths which the Catholic does not question, which, in the nature of things he cannot question and remain a Catholic, there is nothing to prevent his thinking about them, with a view to understanding them a little more clearly. He knows why he believes what he believes, or if he does not he is encouraged to find out. On the whole, priests will complain not that the average Catholic speculates too much, but that he does not enquire sufficiently into the content of his faith. A book such as F. J. Sheed's *Theology and Sanity*, written by a layman, a book which has received an enthusiastic reception wherever it is known, is sufficient to show that Catholics do think and are encouraged to think.

What is true is that the Catholic layman has an immense reverence for the priesthood, and will treat any priest with a respect out of all proportion to his social standing or intellectual attainments. But this is because the believing Catholic sees in the priest the minister of the Sacraments, those channels of life-giving grace of which we have spoken earlier. It is also true that, because the priest has made a special study of theology— it should be borne in mind that the all-but universal rule is for every candidate for the priesthood to spend four years exclusively on the study of different aspects of theology, preceded by two years of philosophy—the layman will listen to his views on those subjects with a becoming modesty. But the layman is just as aware as is the priest himself that, as human beings, they are on the same level of importance in God's eyes, that the priest will have to answer before God for the way in which he has treated the souls entrusted to him. Any misuse of the power that comes to him because of his position as minister of the sacraments clearly savours of sacrilege, and will incur a special punishment. It may be that the uneducated will have an exaggerated opinion of the clever- ness of some priest who is not, from an intellectual standpoint, very impressive, but on the whole they do not bother their heads much about such questions. They are content to know that the priest has undertaken certain obligations which he normally fulfils with exactness and fidelity. There are slack priests as there as slack doctors. But each class should be judged on the generality. So judged, the Catholic priesthood is entitled to the respect and admiration of the world. Its members lead lives of great responsibility—after all they are responsible for the provision of the means whereby souls may hope to come to that knowledge and love of God for which they were created—lives dedicated in a special way to God through the obligation of celibacy imposed on the clergy of the Latin Church.

Some account must here be given of the reasons behind the Church's law of celibacy and the motives which inspire and help the priest in the fulfilment of what is clearly a great undertaking. The main reason behind the growth of this law is undoubtedly the idea of dedication. Already in New Testament times, as we see from St. Paul, the notion was developing that marriage was somehow incompatible with the life of full dedication to the service of God. "The married man is con- cerned with the world's claim, asking how he is to please his wife; and thus he is at issue with the Lord's claim, intent on holiness, bodily and spiritual; whereas the married woman is concerned with the world's claim, asking how she is to please her husband." It is obvious, of course, that the Christian life can be lived in a perfect way in marriage. But it is equally obvious that, in the married state, the complete surrender of each party to the other can become an obstacle to the full practice of the Christian way of life. Even in certain natural lines of action, such as the undertakings of the traveller or explorer, naval officers and the like, there is often a conflict of claims which can be very acute and distressing. Now, where the priest must give himself wholeheartedly to the service of God in others, it becomes an urgent need that he shall somehow be set apart from the exclusive claim of wife and family.

Behind this again is the purely religious and personal idea of the intimacy of union between Christ and the priest who represents him in such an astonishing way. Marriage is, as St. Paul reminds us, a sign of the union existing between Christ and his spouse, the Church. The reality is the Christ-and-Church union; marriage is but the type. Where then there exists such a close bond as that between Christ and his priest, it was felt that there was no room for the mere type to co-exist. The ideal of celibacy and virginity began to be esteemed as an expression of the God-dedicated life. That it is a fitting expression cannot be doubted, although, of course, mere physical virginity without the corresponding interior spirit of dedication carries no spiritual significance. The Catholic cult of virginity then is not to be regarded as a sterile and negative thing. If it is not chosen for the right motive, it is not, in itself, preferable to the self-sacrificing, often heroic, lives led by those in the married state.

Since the fourth century, the Church has consistently acted on the view that the life of the priest requires the vow of celibacy. The law was not universal at first, and it would be idle to deny that it has at times been a source of great difficulty and embarrassment. This is especially true of the tenth and eleventh centuries, when the most strenuous efforts on the part of the ecclesiastical authorities were required to restore something like the practice demanded by the law of the Church. But the fact that, despite all these difficulties, the

Church has continued to insist on the full observance of the law not only shows the high value she places upon it, but also implies that she has never failed to believe in the possibility of its fulfilment. It is a disciplinary matter and the rule is capable therefore of modification. Unless the Church authorities were convinced that the overwhelming majority of her priests could and did remain faithful, she would hardly continue to demand the observance of a rule which must remain a dead letter.

A dispassionate study of the evidence bears out the contention that by the grace of God this high ideal is effectively realised. Occasional scandals come to light, but the very fact that, when revealed, they do cause such horror in the minds of the faithful and such shocked satisfaction in the eyes of the Church's enemies, is sufficient proof of the general integrity of the priesthood as a whole. If further evidence were needed it would be possible to quote the testimony of a man like Renan who, although he severed his connection with the Church and could not therefore feel obliged to defend at all costs an institution in which he no longer believed, declared: "I spent thirteen years of my life under the charge of priests and I never saw the shadow of a scandal; I have known no priests but good priests."

Having spoken of the priesthood, let us now say a word about nuns. The ideal behind their vow of virginity is similar to that which inspires the priest. They wish to belong exclusively to God, to devote themselves to the service of God, and following the teaching of St. Paul they believe that they can best do this by taking the vows of religion, including that of chastity. What has been said of the success of priests in observing their obligations can be asserted with equal confidence of nuns. Despite the scurrilous stories of Bocaccio and the rest, the level of fidelity in this matter is an astonishing tribute to the power of God's grace. Nor should nuns be thought of as either entering convents simply because of being crossed in love or remaining there in a condition of idle and unprofitable morbidity. Nothing could be more misleading. The amount of devoted work accomplished by nuns in the fields of education, nursing and charitable activities of every kind is on a scale that cannot be appreciated by those who have had no first-hand experience of their immense achievement. And in a world where some form of mental instability is becoming more and more common, convents remain distinguished for the wholesomeness and sanity of their inmates. There are to be found crochety and eccentric nuns, as there are to be found crochety and eccentric men and women everywhere. But the incidence of eccentricity in convents is certainly less and probably considerably less than elsewhere. It is clearly not a point that can be proved by statistics, but only by the experience of those who have had average experience of both convent life and life elsewhere. But there is certainly no evidence at all to suggest that nuns as a body have become dehumanised, or that their consecration to God has left them any less ready and able to serve mankind. And in a world which is losing much of the spirit of courtesy and graciousness, convents are amongst the last refuges of good manners and good taste.

But again, although we have discussed and defended the way of life chosen by nuns by an appeal to pragmatic tests there is of course a much deeper significance in that vocation. Nor indeed is it possible to apply such a pragmatic test to, say, the lives of contemplative nuns—those who, living in strict isolation from the world of men, devote themselves to prayer and the contemplation of divine truth; work of course is a part of their daily routine, partly because work is a necessary part of a human existence, partly because they need to support themselves by some such activity. To most men the lives of contemplative nuns are a puzzle and something of a scandal. They incline to echo the words of Stevenson:

> But still the Lord is Lord of might:
> In deeds, in deeds, he takes delight.

What deeds can these point to?

Well, most people would probably admit that, in the end, a man is judged not by what he does but by what he is. The mere external energising is not what really matters. Activity uncontrolled by thought leads to confusion. For the contemplative, thought is prior to activity, God is prior to man, the thought of God prior to work on behalf of man. Yet, precisely because the contemplative nun thus insists on putting first things first, her contribution to man's well-being is of paramount importance. It is well that there be in the world groups of such people reminding us of the things that are to our peace, refusing to be stampeded into activity for the sake of activity, insisting on maintaining a due hierarchy of interests. Certainly the world cannot be said to be suffering from a surfeit of prayer and self-sacrifice. When the final balance comes to be struck, it may well turn out that the great benefactors of the human race have been not its inventors and explorers, its soldiers and men of action, but its contemplative monks and nuns.

In the nature of things they will always be the exception. Those who are moved to impatience at the thought of Trappist monasteries and Carmelite convents, should bear in mind that the overwhelming majority of Catholics are the fathers and mothers of families, members of the professions and factory workers, the ordinary men and women who make up human society everywhere. Indeed, some of the reproach which is levelled at the Church comes from the fact that she is catering for the average man and not the specialist, that whilst she maintains the highest standards of perfection for those who can rise to them, she knows that she must make every allowance for the weakness of human nature and not bind insupportable burdens on the shoulders of her children. The charge of 'casuistry' which is sometimes brought against her is due to the need for adjusting the demands of the moral law to the circumstances of human existence. She will not compromise on the principles; but she is far from a Pharisaic insistence on the letter of the law at the expense of its spirit. Not without justification can she claim that her age-long experience of human nature enables her, under the guidance of the Holy Spirit, to maintain a system of moral teaching in which the rigidity of principle is tempered by a flexibility of application, that the work of her priests is not merely to uphold a moral ideal but also to act in the spirit of Christ who opposed to a soul-destroying legalism a doctrine which, combined with a maintenance of the fullest observance of God's law, a recognition of the loving fatherhood which tempers the wind to the shorn lamb.

This is achieved to a large extent because she instructs more by living example than by arid formulas. The Catholic devotion to the Saints is one of the chief means by which this instruction is realised. Because she is aware that a substantial part of her mission is the sanctification of her children, she naturally concerns herself much with the practical manifestations of sanctity. Whilst many religious bodies are concerned with the improvement of social conditions, with the suppression of vice, with good works of various kinds, she aims at producing in her members that Christ-consciousness and Christ-centredness which is the essential of true sanctity. And an important part of her technique is the practical demonstration of sanctity in action. The type and model of all human sanctity is, of course, Jesus Christ. But because Christ lives on in his members, because in them he reproduces in a myriad ways the rich variety of human perfectability, therefore has the Church, from the beginning, encouraged her children to find inspiration and example from the lives and achievements of outstanding figures amongst those members. It is yet another example of the way in which a common human interest is taken over and used by her for the highest ends. Mankind has found inspiration in the story of great men ever since the day when Homeric rhapsodists sang of the deeds of kings and heroes. In the earliest centuries of the Christian story, the acts of the martyrs were recorded and circulated for the encouragement of the faithful. Soon the lives of those great athletes of Christ were similarly described. Veneration followed on admiration. Gradually the Church found it desirable to control and supervise such veneration, lest unwholesome doctrine or misguided conduct should be held up as ideal.

Eventually the elaborate process of canonization was developed, with its strict rules for the maintenance of high standards of teaching and example. It was Urban VIII (1634) who reserved to the Holy See the power (which had hitherto been enjoyed by local ecclesiastical authority) of granting public honours to martyrs and 'confessors'. Before that there had been some laxity in permitting the honours of sanctity to be paid to some who were hardly worthy of it, because bishops had failed to enquire with sufficient care into the moral qualities of some whom they had permitted their flocks to venerate as saints. In modern times, as is well known, the process leading to the formal canonization of anyone is long and scrupulously careful, amongst other requirements being proof of at least two miracles worked at the intercession of the saint whose cause is being promoted. The evidence for these and for the virtuous lives of the candidate for canonization is scrutinised by competent bodies several times before the cause is allowed to proceed. Eventually, when all requirements have been satisfied, a Bull of Canonization is issued by the Holy Father and at a solemn ceremony in St. Peter's the new Saint is "raised to the altars of the Church," the traditional phrase meaning that public veneration of Saint is enjoined, including Masses in his honour.

CHAPTER NINE

THE ORGANISATION OF THE ROMAN CATHOLIC CHURCH

THE governing body of the Catholic Church, bearing the name of the Catholic Hierarchy, is headed by the Sovereign Pontiff, the Bishop of Rome. He is assisted in the ordinary administration of the affairs of the Church by the Sacred College of Cardinals and the Roman Curia. The local rulers of the different regional sub-divisions are the Patriarchs, Archbishops and Bishops. In addition to these are the Apostolic Delegates, Vicars and Prefects, together with other Prelates whose positions will be described later.

THE POPE

The title itself, which is in common use in the Eastern Church to designate simple priests, was, in the West, originally used of bishops in general, though by the fourth century it had begun to be applied distinctively of the Bishop of Rome. Eventually Gregory VII (1073-1085) decreed that it was to be confined exclusively to the successors of St. Peter. Other titles used of the Pope are *Summus Pontifex*—doubtless with a reminiscence of the Jewish High Priest—*Pontifex Maximus*—a title going back to the days of Pagan Rome—and *Servus Servorum Dei*, 'the Servant of God's servants'. All these were also at one time applied to bishops, but like *Papa* they came to be used specifically of the Head of the Church.

As is well known, the position of the Pope is guaranteed for Roman Catholics by the text: ". . . Thou art Peter and it is upon this rock that I will build my church; and the gates of hell shall not prevail against it; and I will give thee the keys of the kingdom of heaven; whatever thou shalt bind on earth shall be bound in heaven; and whatever thou shalt loose on earth shall be loosed in heaven." (Matt. 16 : 18-19.)

Catholics believe that, in these words, Christ intended to confer upon Peter the supreme power in the church he intended to found, and as that Church was meant to be permanent, they do not doubt that the power so conferred was to be handed on by Peter to his successors. The terms 'bind' and 'loose' are taken from the current terminology of the Jewish Rabbinical schools, and connote legislative and judicial authority. The authority is, of course, limited to the spiritual sphere, being concerned with the kingdom of heaven. But in that sphere it is absolute. To Peter and to Peter alone is given 'the power of the keys'. In all that concerns the affairs of the Church, including such material possessions as may be needful for her spiritual activity, the ultimate authority is the Pope.

In theory, then, the authority of the Pope is that of an absolute monarch. Yet it is true to say that never was there an authority which was exercised with a greater sense of responsibility. For the Pope himself is aware that, unlimited as his powers may seem to be, he will be required to give the strictest account of them to the Master from whom he has received them. In virtue of their very nature, he is constantly reminded of the Master who "did not come to have service done to him: he came to serve others . . ." (Mark 10 : 45.) Amongst the many titles possessed by the Pope, not the least veracious is that which describes him as *Servus Servorum*. In the vast structure of administrative machinery and canon law, in the manifold richness of Catholic practice and external splendour, there can be no sort of doubt that the humblest Catholic looks to the Pope as a true father, the repository for him of the life-giving love of Christ. The fact that the Pope's jurisdiction is described as 'immediate'—that is to say, exercised directly without the need for any mediation—is seen rather as implying the possibility of immediacy of access and appeal, should the occasion ever arise.

The departments in which the jurisdiction of the Pope is exercised are indeed manifold. He is, in the first place, the supreme teacher of the Church, charged with the mission of defining or precising the content of the Catholic Faith, in virtue of his prerogative of Infallibility. Once more it will be necessary to clarify a term which is not seldom misunderstood.

Now it is clear to the Catholic, from the words of Christ already quoted, that some sort of supervision or guarantee has been promised to the Church to keep her from misrepresenting the teaching of her Master. If she is charged with the business of teaching the world 'to observe all the commandments' which Christ has given her, if the 'gates of hell are not to prevail against' her, if he is 'with' her always, if 'he that hears' her hears him, it would seem to follow—and the Catholic has no difficulty in drawing the conclusion—that there must be some sort of assurance that she will not demand assent to teachings which are not, in fact, consonant with the teaching of Christ. And it is precisely this that Infallibility means. It does not mean that the Church or the Pope as her head is gifted with supreme intuitions, endowed with superhuman prudence or intelligence, so that in no circumstances whatsoever can a mistake be made. It does not mean that the Church or the Pope claims to know the answers to all the questions. It is a strictly limited gift, involving nothing more than the claim that when the Pope, speaking officially as Christ's representative on some question of faith or moral principle, makes some pronouncement to be accepted by the whole Church, he is safeguarded by the Holy Spirit from making a mistake. As Mr. Shaw, with some inaccuracy but with much spirit has expressed it: "Perhaps I had better inform my Protestant readers that the famous Dogma of Papal Infallibility is by far the most modest pretension of the kind in existence. Compared to our infallible democracies, our infallible medical councils, our infallible astronomers, our infallible judges, and our infallible parliaments, the Pope is on his knees in the dust confessing his ignorance before the throne of God, asking only that as to certain historical matters on which he has clearly more sources of information open to him than anyone else his decision shall be taken as final."*

It should be pointed out also that, whilst the ultimate pronouncement or definition comes from the Pope individually, that does not mean that it is not preceded by an immense quantity of investigation, consultation and expert advice. Invariably the topic has been thrashed out by theologians

*Preface to *Saint Joan*.

during centuries of debate and examination. For example, the doctrine of the Immaculate Conception, formally defined in 1854, had been almost universally held by the whole Catholic body since the Middle Ages. It is implicit in one passage of the Council of Trent and a liturgical feast implying faith in the doctrine has long been part of the Church's worship.

And of course, whilst Catholics as a body will respect the pronouncements of the Pope on matters not concerning faith or morals, they know perfectly well that there is no sort of guarantee that his judgment in the political field is not as liable to error as is that of any other man. They believe indeed that he has sources of information which are not open to them and that, his position being what it is, he is not likely to make such a pronouncement without good reason. But they do not feel themselves bound by it in conscience, nor do they suppose that it may not some day be reversed.

So much then for the position of the Pope as teacher of the universal Church. But in addition to his positive pronouncements, which are rare enough, there are a number of ancillary activities, such as the condemnation of erroneous views put forward by teachers and writers (though, clearly, these may involve Infallibility), the establishment of universities, the prescription of suitable courses of study, books and other means to the propagation of truth. Not of course that these activities are the personal task of the Pope himself. They are the function of the appropriate Roman departments, as we shall see later.

Closely associated with his office of teacher is his power in the sphere of worship. The liturgical services of the Church, the use of non-liturgical 'devotions', the canonization of saints, the establishment of new festivals, these are some of the many ways in which he controls the activities of Catholics in their public approach to God. This might seem at first sight an unwarrantable interference with the private religious life of the individual, but in fact in his private relations with his Creator the Catholic enjoys considerable freedom. The control of public worship is inevitable because such public acts almost inevitably involve theological positions. Into the formularies of prayer, pictorial representations of Christ or the Saints, and other manifestations, theological implications or statements easily enter. And in any case it is necessary that there be some controlling authority to ensure that the business of worship be carried on in a decent and dignified way.

Of the legislative power of the Pope it is unnecessary to speak in any detail. It is perhaps worth while to insist that all the Church's legislation is meant to safeguard the liberty and the conscience of individual members, although it is inevitable in any institution that the general good must sometimes be realised through the sacrifice of individual liberty. But there is this important difference between the Church and other institutions that, since her end and purpose is the eternal well-being of her subjects, that well-being should be the pre-dominant preoccupation of her rulers, and that a tyrannical exercise of power does not necessarily defeat the end for which power was conferred. Mistaken decisions and acts of harshness may and do occur. The Catholic has the profound satisfaction of knowing that, in spite of all, so long as his conscience is clear, a greater good may come to him through the very injustice that is being done to him. But again—and it is one more sign that the Church is more than human—the confidence which the average Catholic feels in the government of his Church is all but unshakeable.

This section may well close with a brief discussion of the method of election of the Papacy. It should be premised that election to the Bishopric of Rome is election to the Papal throne. In the earliest days of the Church appointment to any bishopric was normally by popular election. The clergy and faithful constituting the local church would assemble to choose one of their number to succeed to the vacant See. The candidate thus elected would then be consecrated by neighbouring bishops and continuity thus secured. The modern practice is for bishops to be appointed by the Supreme Pontiff; he himself however is elected by the College of Cardinals. This is a survival of the democratic election of the earliest times. We have an account of the election of St. Cornelius (251 A.D.) from the pen of St. Cyprian: "He was made bishop by the decree of God and of his Church, by the witness of nearly all the clergy, by the college of aged bishops (*sacerdotum*) and of good men." The freedom of election has frequently suffered from the interference of temporal sovereigns, but the Church has always striven to keep such pressure as far as possible from influencing her decision.

On the death of the Pope, then, a Conclave of all Cardinals is summoned at Rome. The greatest precautions are taken to keep the electors secluded from contact with the outside world so as to prevent improper pressure being brought to bear and the seclusion continues until one candidate receives the necessary two-thirds majority of all votes cast. The choice normally but not necessarily falls upon a member of the Sacred College.

The College of Cardinals

The history of the development of the College of Cardinals, interesting as it is, is far too complicated for adequate treatment here. It must suffice to give the briefest sketch. Derived from the Latin word *cardo* meaning a hinge, the term *cardinal* was originally applied to any priest permanently attached to a church; it was then used of one belonging to a central or episcopal church; eventually it was restricted to clerics belonging to the church at Rome—the hinge of the universal Church. Here the rank and style of cardinal was conferred not merely on priests but also on bishops and deacons. The cardinal bishops, originally, it would seem, called upon by the Pope to deputise for him at episcopal functions, soon came to act as a small advisory council. They each have a diocese in the immediate vicinity of Rome. The cardinal-priests, originally the senior priests of the Roman churches and responsible for ecclesiastical discipline in the city, are now drawn from all over the world, being almost invariably bishops with their own dioceses. But each, on appointment, receives a 'titular' church in Rome. Finally come the cardinal-deacons, historically deriving from the seven deacons responsible for the care of the poor in the seven Roman regions.

The Sacred College, when its numbers are complete, contains seventy members, six cardinal-bishops, fifty cardinal-priests and fourteen cardinal-deacons. The senior cardinal-bishop is dean of the Sacred College and is always bishop of

Ostia. It is his privilege to consecrate the new Pope. The senior cardinal-deacon similarly proclaims and crowns him. All cardinals are 'created' by the Sovereign Pontiff, personally.

THE ROMAN CURIA

The different departments of the Papal administrative service constitute the Roman Curia. It is impossible here even to enumerate them all but it is necessary to indicate their general character by choosing a few typical specimens. Thus the Congregation of the Holy Office, of which the Pope is Prefect and a Cardinal-bishop secretary, is concerned with the general task of watching over the purity of faith and moral teaching in the Church. Before it come charges of heretical doctrine and it is responsible for the examination and condemnation of dangerous books. The Consistorial Congregation, of which again the Pope is Prefect, with a Cardinal-priest as secretary, is chiefly concerned with the erection and division of dioceses, the appointment of bishops, the reports of bishops concerning the state of their dioceses and similar matters. The Congregation for the Eastern Church and that for the Affairs of Religious (i.e., members of religious orders) sufficiently explain themselves, whilst the Congregation 'de Propaganda Fide' is primarily concerned with missionary countries, in which a full hierarchy has not yet been established. Others again deal with Sacred Rites and with Seminaries and Universities. In all there are twelve such Congregations. There are also three Tribunals, of which the best known is the Rota— the Roman court of law—and six offices, including the Secretariate of State.

PATRIARCHATES AND DIOCESES

Under the central government established in Rome, the administration of the Church is largely carried on through the smaller units known as dioceses, a term which takes us back to the reorganisations of the Roman Empire carried out by Diocletian at the end of the third century. There still survive in the Middle East a small number of patriarchates, of which the most historic are those of Jerusalem and Antioch, Alexandria and Constantinople. In general the rule is for a number of dioceses to be grouped together, though a bishop is strictly speaking responsible to the Holy See alone. In many cases, a bishop is assisted by an Auxiliary or Coadjutor, with a 'titular' See, situated in some region not under the jurisdiction of Rome.

Under the archbishop or bishop is the parish priest, owing obedience to him and responsible to him for the administration of the parish entrusted to him. In larger parishes, the parish priest may be assisted by as many as six curates.

It is of course through the activities of the parish organisation that the ordinary Catholic is most aware of the Church as living fact. At the same time, by his periodic visitations, the bishop of the diocese keeps in touch with local activities and organisations, whilst he himself, through his visits to Rome, to report in person to the Holy See provides a link between his parochial clergy and their parishioners on the one side and the majestic and historic centre of the universal Church on the other.

In missionary lands, where the regular hierarchical organisation has not yet been established, it is customary for affairs to be managed by Vicars or Prefects Apostolic. Apostolic Delegates are generally appointed to represent the Holy See either on some special mission or as permanent officials with quasi-diplomatic status.

THE RELIGIOUS ORDERS

Falling outside the regular hierarchical organisation of the Church, though in complete subordination to the Holy See, are the Religious Orders. To understand their nature and function it will be necessary to sketch briefly the story of their development. In the early centuries of the history of the Church, in pursuit of the ideal of complete renunciation of the world, men lived eremitical lives, chiefly in the deserts of Egypt and Syria. At first the movement was completely individualistic and unorganised, but by the beginning of the fourth century, chiefly through the inspiration and instruction of St. Anthony, something like a regular rule of life began to appear. Soon the hermits began to group together in loose communities, uniting especially for prayer and worship. The Egyptian monk Pacomius (about 340 A.D.) founded what was perhaps the first monastery in the Upper Thebaid, but it was St. Basil of Cappadocia who first formulated anything like a detailed Rule.

From the East, the idea of living a life of Christian perfection away from the ordinary circumstances of family and civic organisation spread to the West, and towards the end of the fourth century, under the influence of men like Ambrose, Martin of Tours and Jerome, monasteries began to be established on the islands off the West coast of Italy and the Southern coast of Gaul. Even in the cities of Italy and Gaul monastic establishments came into existence. But it was through the work of Benedict of Nursia that Western Monasticism finally realised itself. His foundation at Monte Cassino in the early decades of the sixth century was the forerunner of those innumerable centres of piety and civilisation which did more than any other institution to keep alive in the darkest ages the fire of culture and humanity.

By this time the general principles of the religious life had become fixed. The essentials were the three vows of poverty, chastity and obedience by which the monk surrendered all right to own property, to enjoy marriage, to determine his own career. Every detail of his life was arranged for him by his superiors, whose commands he regarded as expressing the will of God for him. At the same time, this was no merely negative life of self-denial. His day was filled with the *Opus Dei*, the great work of singing the praises of God in the choral recitation of the Divine Office and with manual or literary activity, clearing the forest lands and cultivating the soil or preserving for posterity the literary products of ancient civilisation.

Successive modifications of the Benedictine Rule brought into being the different types of Orders—Carthusians, Cistercians, Trappists—basically similar in ideal but each with its characteristic contribution to the development of monasticism. It is from the ranks of the monks that the great Churchmen, scholars and saints of the age were drawn. The spread of Christianity in central and northern Europe was largely due to them. At a time when the reputation of the papacy was at its lowest, it was the monks of the west who maintained and developed the highest ideals of Christian conduct. It was a monk—Gregory VII—who was to show himself most filled with zeal for the reform of the Church.

At the beginning of the thirteenth century two new names appear. Dominic and Francis founded the Orders which are popularly named after them, the former to preach the word of God in an age of heresy and ignorance, the latter to live in a more striking way than ever that life of poverty which Christ demands of his closest followers. And again it was from the religious orders, supremely from the Dominicans but also in important measure from the Franciscans that the great philosophers and theologians of the mediæval Church arose. There were others of course who were not religious; but the names of Thomas Aquinas the Dominican and the Franciscan Duns Scotus will suffice to justify the generalisation.

The next great foundation comes in the sixteenth century with the establishment of the Society of Jesus. Since that day there have been founded orders and congregations too numerous even to catalogue, each instituted to meet some particular need yet all alike in the insistence of the essentials of religious life. In many ways, indeed, their very activities are indistinguishable, so that in England at the present day Benedictines, Dominicans, Jesuits and others are found active in the work of education; Benedictines, Dominicans, Franciscans, Jesuits, Redemptorists and others are found working side by side with the parochial clergy in the everyday routine of parish work. In the special department of parish work, religious no less than 'secular' clergy come under the jurisdiction of the Bishop, since the care of souls is ultimately his responsibility. But in all that is peculiar to religious life, the members of religious orders owe allegiance not to the Bishop but to their own superiors and through them to the Pope. Thus, side by side with the hierarchical organisation which we have studied above, is as it were another hierarchy.

Take for example the organisation of the Society of Jesus. Its 29,000 members are grouped into some fifty provinces, according to national and geographical divisions. At the head of each Province is the Provincial, who is responsible for a group of schools, churches and other establishments, each in its turn governed by its local superior. At Rome resides the General, to whom all the Provincials owe obedience and who is advised in his work by a Curia of Assistants, representatives of different groups of Provinces. The General himself, like the least of his subjects, is subordinate to the authority of the Holy See. So is it with the other religious orders. Different as they may be in immediate aim, organisation or way of life, anomalous as they may seem to be by the side of the symmetry of the Church's hierarchical organisation, they all yet collaborate and coalesce in their devotion to the cause of Christ and his Vicar on earth.

MEMBERSHIP AND RECRUITMENT OF THE CHURCH

Membership of the Church comes through Baptism. It is the normal practice for the children of Catholic parents to be baptized within a month of birth. Such parents who are responsible for the entry into existence of a human being, will wish that human being to have what they regard as the supremely important gift of supernatural life. In a sense, this might seem to be committing the child to a way of life that it cannot yet appreciate. But that is in keeping with the universal law by which we are all committed to life itself without any choice on our part. We are born into a certain environment. It is our duty and our destiny to make the most of the gift of life. So is it the high responsibility of the Catholic child as he grows to manhood to assimilate himself to the faith which he has thus received as the gift of God. Not all succeed—whether through their own fault or not God alone can judge—and Catholics regard it as the supreme tragedy when one of their number 'loses the faith'.

Equally of course they rejoice when, as not infrequently happens, non-Catholics receive the gift of faith. This joy is due far more to the unselfish desire to see others possessing the riches of that faith than to any mere institutional vanity. Believing as they do that it is God's will that all men should come to a knowledge of the truth, convinced as they are that the truth is revealed most completely in the Church, Catholics are naturally eager to preach that truth to others. As they see it, it is the way to implement their daily prayer: Thy Kingdom come.

THE CATHOLIC HIERARCHY

The Sovereign Pontiff

Pius XII (Eugenio Pacelli): born in Rome, March 2, 1876; elected Pope, March 2; crowned, March 12, 1939.

Cardinals

The Sacred College of Cardinals numbers not more than seventy, of whom not more than seven are Cardinal-bishops, occupying the suburbican Sees of Rome: there are some fifty titular churches in Rome, to be allotted as required to Cardinal-priests, whilst the remaining members of the Sacred College are Cardinal-deacons.

Patriarchal Sees

Latin Rite	8 in number
Oriental Rites (in union with the See of Rome)..	6
Archiepiscopal Sees	369
Episcopal Sees	1,024
'Titular' Sees (occupied by auxiliary bishops)	750
Missionary countries are administered by	
Apostolic Delegations	17
Apostolic Vicariates	324
or Apostolic Prefectures	132

In addition, in some countries, as in England, the Holy See has a special diplomatic representative—an Apostolic Delegate or a Nuncio.

In Great Britain, the number of Archbishops or Bishops is thirty-four, the number of priests approximately 8,000. The number of Roman Catholics is approximately 3,000,000.

The total number of Roman Catholics in the world is estimated at 300,000,000.

SELECT BIBLIOGRAPHY

GENERAL: For those who would like a more extended treatment of certain questions than has been possible here, probably the most useful work is *The Catholic Encyclopædia* ("an international work of reference on the constitution, doctrine, discipline and history of the Catholic Church") in sixteen volumes. (Caxton Publishing Co., London, 1907, etc.)

Short, popular works recommended are: *The Life of the Church* (Edited by M. C. D'Arcy: Sheed & Ward, 1932) and the *Spirit of Catholicism* by Karl Adam (Eng. trans. Sheed & Ward, 1934). An invaluable discussion of the historical development of the Church prior to the Middle Ages is *The Making of Europe* by Christopher Dawson (Sheed & Ward, 1932).

THEOLOGY: For those who need a full scholarly treatment, the *Dictionnaire de Théologie catholique*, edited by Vacant and Mangenot, is outstanding. Good short outlines are numerous, one of the latest and best being F. J. Sheed's *Theology and Sanity* (Sheed & Ward, 1947).

Information about the Catholic Church in England at the present day is to be found in *The Catholic Directory*, published annually by Burns & Oates.

INDEX